pinchbeck ~~en~~ enisled

draperies 160 - blac[illegible] ed ste[illegible] trusses [illegible] ambient catenaries

W9-CTY-812

v 99 New York – Most of the humor falls flat – a shallow poem

vvv 95 The Loss of Smyrna (brilliant formal poem of debauchery's dreams and ultimate failure

vv 90 The Muse in the Monkey Tower

vv 50 Collected Novels

vv 156 The Ninth of AB good poem about his summers away from the city

48 vv Nocturne – The mysterious woman Anima of the city

vv Helicon – a very Touching ~~po~~ memory of his days at Columbia and giving blood with Allen Ginsberg – towards The end he says, vv "I have bled since To many cadences" The last line, however, is a little weak

vv 120 At The New Year (my circle poem)

vv 117 Ad Musam gifts to a lover

154 Humming (summer & cicadas)

vvvv 167 From The Ramble Brilliant, Mallarméan poem about femininity and nature in the form of three sister pools in Central Park

21 questing after new Quests

girl of air page 14

2026 poem 32 33 ?

BOOKS BY JOHN HOLLANDER

Poetry

Spectral Emanations: New and Selected Poems 1978
Reflections on Espionage 1976
Tales Told of the Fathers 1975
The Head of the Bed 1974
Town and Country Matters 1972
The Night Mirror 1971
Types of Shape 1969
Visions from the Ramble 1965
Movie-Going 1962
A Crackling of Thorns 1958

Criticism

Vision and Resonance 1975
Two Senses of Poetic Form
The Untuning of the Sky 1961
Ideas of Music in English Poetry 1500–1700

For Children

The Immense Parade on Supererogation Day and What Happened to It 1972
The Quest of the Gole 1966

Spectral Emanations

New and Selected Poems

clavichord

Spectral Emanations

New and Selected Poems

By John Hollander

Atheneum *New York* 1978

The new poems in this collection originally appeared in the following periodicals, some in slightly different form:

THE NEW YORKER: *Spectral Emanations* (*Blue; Indigo*)*;* Copyright © 1975 and 1976 by The New Yorker Magazine, Inc.
THE NEW REPUBLIC: *The Lady of the Castle;* Copyright © 1974 by The New Republic
THE NEW YORK REVIEW OF BOOKS: *Collected Novels; Here is the Sun: the Summer Afternoon is Hot With Wasps; The Angler's Story;* Copyright © 1975 and 1976 by The New York Review of Books
POETRY: *Spectral Emanations* (*Orange; Yellow; prose commentary on Indigo; Violet*)*;* Copyright © 1976 by Poetry
THE TIMES LITERARY SUPPLEMENT: *Nocturne; Looking East on Twelfth Street*

Poems from the following previously published books are included in the present volume:

A CRACKLING OF THORNS, copyright © 1958 by Yale University Press
MOVIE-GOING AND OTHER POEMS, copyright © 1958, 1959; 1960, 1961, 1962 by John Hollander
VISIONS FROM THE RAMBLE, copyright © 1962, 1963, 1964, 1965 by John Hollander
TYPES OF SHAPE, copyright © 1967, 1968, 1969 by John Hollander
THE NIGHT MIRROR, copyright © 1966, 1967, 1968, 1969, 1970, 1971 by John Hollander
TOWN AND COUNTRY MATTERS, copyright © 1972 by John Hollander
TALES TOLD OF THE FATHERS, copyright © 1975 by John Hollander

Library of Congress catalog card number 77–20645
ISBN 0–689–10888–5 (cloth)
0–689–10878–8 (paperback)
Published simultaneously in Canada by McClelland and Stewart Ltd.
Manufactured by American Book–Stratford Press, Inc.,
Saddle Brook, New Jersey
Designed by Harry Ford
First Edition

For Harry and Kathleen

CROSSING WATER

"August, 1946: Back from Nantucket on the upper deck of the ferry. A hot night, scraps of light remaining in the sky, as if of a few high lengths of cloud, long after sunset. I do not concern myself with their location astern—which is rather peculiar for residual light of that kind—nor with the utter darkness of the west into which we are headed. There is laughter from the deck below, a quiet continual throbbing of buried engines and the hoarse breathing of our wash. I stand at the starboard rail, sadly shunning others. Then the rags of radiance above awaken, yawn, stretch, gradually gather themselves into long pale bolts and begin to unroll slowly and extravagantly. Some are greenish, some are the bluish white of heavy drapery, flicked by the passing shoulder of something vast into waves that move forward yet do not advance. Then the fingers of cold dull red begin to grope for the zenith, pointing into it and pushing it farther away. The sky is wild with their light . . ."

———*All of this went on and on, finally growing pale seemingly at the same rate at which all the motion slowed eventually, colors fading into a glowing dimness against the dark, until, at a moment that could have come along almost anywhere during the period of five minutes it marked the middle of, a long slow streak of white meteor shot through the pallor above, a gasp of luminosity, a revision of wonder and a reduction of what had been seen to be a sign. Ironic, clear, distinct; vector of agency against a scene; short, pointed, a stretch of high path heading downward . . . well, I was young and foolish and unable to know—as with everything else I had ever been given —the nature of the gift. The bright track of the Perseid was short, but long enough to lead into the vast space of darkness between sky and sea. It has taken me thirty years to remember the mockery of its accidence, thirty years to recompose the prior light.*

CONTENTS

NEW POEMS

FROM TALES TOLD OF THE FATHERS (*1975*)

FROM TOWN AND COUNTRY MATTERS (*1972*)

FROM THE NIGHT MIRROR (*1971*)

FROM TYPES OF SHAPE (*1968*)

FROM VISIONS FROM THE RAMBLE (*1965*)

FROM MOVIE-GOING AND OTHER POEMS (*1962*)

FROM A CRACKLING OF THORNS (*1958*)

New Poems

Spectral Emanations

A Poem in Seven Branches in Lieu of a Lamp

"There was a meaning and purpose in each of its seven branches, and such a candlestick cannot be lost forever. When it is found again, and seven lights are kindled and burning in it, the whole world will gain the illumination which it needs. Would not this be an admirable idea for a mystic story or parable, or seven-branched allegory, full of poetry, art, philosophy, and religion? It shall be called 'The Recovery of the Sacred Candlestick.' As each branch is lighted, it shall have a differently colored lustre from the other six; and when all seven are kindled, their radiance shall combine into the white light of truth."

The golden lamp of the Second Temple in Jerusalem, borne into Rome in the triumph of Titus, probably did not fall off the Milvian bridge when Constantine saw in the sky the sign by which he would conquer. The text which follows intends to hoist up another lamp from other waters than those of the Tiber. Lost bronze is silent, let alone lost gold; even the newest oil has no echo. I have here kindled the lights of sound, starting with the red cry of battle, followed by the false orange gold, true yellow goldenness, the green of all our joy, blue of our imaginings, the indigo between and the final violet that is next to black, for that is how our scale runs. Below each cup of color is a branch of prose, following and supporting it. Only at the moment of green is there time for a story, for only that branch is vertical, the other supports being parabolic. This is in memory of my father,

Franklin Hollander, 1899–1966.

5

PROLOGUE

THE WAY TO THE THRONE ROOM

On the captive shore, the bright river hard by, this happened: I had seen what I had seen, and I had come to the gates.

At the gate, questions were put. As: *Who poured the oil? Penemue,* I allowed, *the breather inside. He who taught me to know the bitter from the sweet, and how to write with ink and paper.*

As: *Who trimmed the wick? Gananiel,* I confessed, *the lopper of branches, the one who limits that the many may flourish. Surely he did it.*

As: *Who struck a light? Bhel,* I reconstructed, *the starred one, that we may see, that we may write our poor books, white fire on black fire.*

As: *Who kindled the flames? Puriel,* I suggested, *the melter and blender who cast the cups of fiery gold and then cupped the golden fire.*

As: *Who raised his hands toward the burning? Why, Roy G. Biv,* I snorted, *the man of lead, though his melting point was low, Roy G. Biv.*

As: *Who wept at the light? O, I did,* I chanted, *or at least I did when I remembered the radiance.*

As: *Who ended it all? Dr. Hitson, the awakener,* I screamed, *he blew out the flames at the end—with an explosion of violent force.*

Then I halted at the cold gates. Statues waited at wide intervals along the courtyard, disposed in flexions of the usual; their faces were blank, all waiting to be carved. All dreamed.

Then the gate opened and I was led through the court, through the glowing opened portal, through the dimmed hall, its vast walls hung with fringes.

On the way to the first chamber, dark, polished teakwood shone, as if in the falling rainwater. Those who looked wonderingly at it and saw an otter were not admitted.

On the way to the second chamber, the lighter and the darker woods mottled each other, braided with interlace. No one who cried out as if at an adder was permitted to pass.

On the way to the third chamber, the walls were leathern and darkened gold. Those who fancied that the smell of earth was there were all turned away.

On the way to the fourth chamber, strange pictures hung: a glass of green fur, an open apple, a house of loss; and portraits of the Baron of Grass, the Count of Nought. Those who approached to read the titles had to go all the way back.

On the way to the fifth chamber, all was smooth and slate, as if beauty were a disease of surface, an encroachment of depth. Many fell asleep, and had to be removed.

On the way to the sixth chamber, everything was mirrored, yea even to mirroring itself. Those who felt within them even the faintest twitch of answering light were struck blind.

7

On the way to the seventh chamber, the amethyst and sapphire light ceased and there were glimmering marble slabs. They dazzled mine eyes, and it was not at my own tears that I cried out *O water! Water!* Thus I was never to enter.

RED

Along the wide canal
Vehement, high flashings
Of sunlight reflect up
From rock, from bunker, from
Metal plate. In the mild
Shade of his waiting place—
Shade a gourd might afford—
J sits embracing his
Automatic weapon,
Crowned by a sloppy cap,
Inhaling the fire of
White air from the parched east.

J is exceedingly
Glad of the gourd—of his
Arp-shaped drop of shadow,
Its eye-shaped stain—but the
Flashings have prepared a
Worm of white fire, blazing
With an unseen pain the
Whites of his eyes to blank.
Red winds lash his throat, then
Blood bubbles into milk,
Shit and pale viscera
Drop into soured honey.

Into the morning fire,
Into the white fighting,

Tender olive bird plucked
Out of Leviathan,
Out of a statehood, grim
And necessary, he
Has hung through the unjust
Noon, fire at his right hand,
The fierce ghost of his sire;
At his left, waiting to
Stain its flames to crimson,
Dark of his bloody dam.

For forty winks in the
Desert, his eyelids clank
Down. Then, the fiery worm:
Unwilling prophet of
His past, he sees screaming
Seals ripped open, vision
Uncurling, as can by
Opened can the film of
The ages runs in coils
Across his mind's sky: Bronze
Spears smash grayware pitchers,
Torches splash fear near tents;

Slow, greaved legs clang along
Parasangs of gray road;
Brave and fair embrace the
Bad and dark; arrows snap
Against square parapets;
Sons of the desert rise;
Gray, wreathed heads lock crowns on
Blond curls; the bright tower
Is truly taken; there
Are kingdoms, there are songs
Along the wall———but his
Films melt into jelly:

9

Now at his red moment
He forgets his city
As his tongue is made to
Fuck the roof of his mouth,
His skull cradling little
Ones of brain is dashed now
Against rock, and the pulp
Of him slips to the ground.
Blood, rooted in earth, makes
Adam's kingdom, Adom,
Fruit brought forth of iron,
The wide realm of the red.

Ox, door, water—these huge simples of our life become red in the grounding sun, stained with the same red. Through the door we see the ox awaiting water. Our pottery is red with black figures of valor. Our ploughshares are honed for tomorrow; by the door, the wooden yoke is grim with nails.

Here at our crimson heroic, the painter images us by dipping into his pot of primaries; the singer keeps returning to *a*.

But we know the color of our bordering flame to arise from the warm deepening of yellow, from the cold intensifying of azure. The darkened line of sun and sky is our rim of blood.

Thus we are always at our westernmost here. If our light goes out, let the rest of you beware.

By night, a red one meanders among the starfields, gathering eyefulls of light: not the Warrior, but the bloodied Saturn, suffused with lateness.

By day, the iron sickle leans against the wall; ringing around a pot, its blade reddens with rust.

By twilight in the courtyard, a pool of water lies quietly cupped in a block of dented stone; in its red mirror the sky, the turreted wall and a peering, eyeing head all are reddened, as in the ambient light of the Last Day.

The red singer sits looking back toward the violet becoming black. His songs are capable of the opened and the spilled; only for them the wind sings in his hair. He stands outside the door: his shadow falls across it. Blown dust makes a false threshold.

ORANGE

The age of awakening: bright
With drops from the crushed, segmented
Sun, the rising hemisphere of
Huge Florida orange. As the
Jupiter Home Juice Extractor
Recoils from its pressures, the dross
Of pulp and rind remain, and the
Innocent air of unhurried
Cold morning widens. But not with
Promises: for nothing adverse
Has ever occurred; promises
That it is never to happen
Need not yet have been invented.
The ear of air is widened by
The sounds of so very many
Individual energies!
They are hoarding light as from the
Traffic of their exaltation
Arises the tone of bright horns
Filling air and aureate ear
With hearsay of the threshing-out
Of gain. Windows facing eastward

Burn with a pale orange fire, as
If loss were being flamed away.

Drops of orange juice that Midas
Thirsts for are turned into burning
Bullets; later on he will be
Trapped inside a cunt of metal,
Pinched for his silly pains by the
Hard parody of flesh into
Which the soft parts of a person
Freeze at his caress. But what of
The God's touch in the Age of Cold?
—Frail Danaë, guarded only
By brazen contrivances, lies
Back, open to the god of gold
Who comes like coins thumbed into her
Slot: squish, chunk. He spends; they melt in
Her; the god has got his hero,
The daughter of brass alloyed, her
Mortality bought, with massy
Gold. Not with the juice of sunlight
Streaming with magnificence does
The crude chrysomorph enter her,
But like light interred in the hard
Shining that dazzles poor eyes with
Mere models of the immortal.

But these fables from the fountain
Of the age of orange themselves
Harden, and the grayer stages
Of the day we create by our
Separations—the juice from the
Crushed vessel of shell, the refined
Metal from the crusty rock—are
Even at best the residues
Of arising. When we heed the

Silly fictions—choosing the lead
Above the gold, the chevelure
Over the brocade—we make our
Moral from the living dullard
Of daylight, not the gleaming dead
God. Here in the gloaming of the
Ages of His Images, we
Pluck the orange flower, or press
The arrant philtre and with a
Midas touch of tongue proclaim an
Oral gold, like Circe turning
Everything of worth into the
Travesty of value, and like
The god putting off the golden,
Squeezing out of it the gold.

"Orange dies out in the ascending fire," roared our grayish remainder; "Gold is a dream of lead," said Roy G. Biv.

When gold can be alloyed to form a working metal, then the Order of Ages will be changed. "But only when it is as common as copper," retorted the stupid jewel of the floor; "Only when it is as dull as lead," said Roy G. Biv.

"Gold is gold," say the sages. "Lead is lead," say the thieves. "What's lead is gold and what's gold is lead," says Roy G. Biv.

All the colors are fractions of white. All the colors burn up in the unseen higher vibrations of glory. "But when I muddied them all in a sty of pigments, when I put them all in the dish and mixed and mixed, all I got was the leaden tone of earth," said Roy G. Biv.

The gleaming of their ruined gold outlasts the kingdoms. "But the mud and the rock around it will prevail," insists the lustreless plumber; "Hurrah for the dull," says Roy G. Biv.

After the gold, the dross; after the juice, the cracked shell; after the emptying, the hollow. "Ah, yes," sighed Rex Cloacarum; "That's me," said Roy G. Biv.

The painter said: "If one were to imagine a bluish orange, it would have to feel like a southwesterly north wind." "No, that would be a reddish green," said the other painter. "It is all the same to me," said Roy G. Biv.

Blessed art thou who bringest forth fruit of the bronze: bells and pomegranates, thunder and lightning. Blessed are thou who brought forth nought of the lead, save Roy G. Biv.

YELLOW

Dirty gold sublimed from the black earth up
In bright air: these are the awaited stalks,
The ripeness possible to imagine
Even among mezzotints of winter,
And to remember having imagined
Oddly amid late spring's lackadaisies
And all of the earlier primulas.
Prophetic pale flecks of forsythia
Lemony against the cold engravings
Of gray branches—these whisper of golden
Flashings over the surface of water
Above the attentive images of
Jonquils peering out at themselves along
The wide bank. Which would be no fulfillment
In any event, of early pallor:
It would remain an interpretation
Of the flimsy text, half unremembered,
Dimming evermore and diminishing.

Like gold afire in the yellow candles'
Flame, steady with remembrances and now
And then only wavering in regret,
What might have been burns up and the bright fruit
Of what we after all have ever ripens.
The squinting flames eye each other as fruit
And flame and eye and yellowy flower.
To have been kept, to have reached this season,
Is to have eternized, for a moment,
The time when promise and fulfillment feed
Upon each other, when the living gold
Of sunlight struck from the amazing corn
Seems one with its cold, unending token,
The warm time when both seem reflections from
The bright eyes of the Queen of the Peaceful
Day being welcomed with these twin burnings,
These prophetic seeds of the Ripener,
Brightness rising and getting on with things.

Or: In the air there is a soft gleaming
As of fair light in certain hair, and wind
Through the pale curtains streaming like moonlight
In the dark air that fills all the rooms of
Dreaming like a perfumed tune that will ne'er . . .
(Vanish? A snuffed lamp in the dream of day?)
This has been all of silver. But see now:
The man of earth exhales a girl of air,
Of her light who lies beside him, gentle
And bare, under the living shawl of all
Her long hair, while her short below softly
Touches his tired thigh with welcoming.
It is that she is there. It is the pure
Return of everlastingness in her
Hands and the readiness of the sweet pear
In the touch of her mouth that fill the air
—Even the air within the circle of

His emptied arms—with light beyond seeming.

The possible metal underwater,
Beer-can or amulet, its reflections
More important than those of the surface
(Remember those jonquils we had before),
This is one thing: but another matter
Is of the precious glare in eloquent
Watery surfaces—in them, but not
Of them. And all that matters in the end
Is of the moment of late, fine morning
When the world's yellow is of burning sands
Leading down to the penultimate blue
Of, say, the Ionian Sea whose waves
Gave light that had to have been of their own
And which, when darkened momently by the
Cool shadows of our gaze, plucked up the deep
Hues of our gleaming feet at the bottom
Of our golden bodies in their purest
And most revealing element at last.

All the eternal ornaments set down in dust will never live nor yet give birth. Pale, unenduring petals go to brown and therefore live in the soft mines of earth. EPHRAIM DU BLÉ ENGRENIER

The leaves ripen for the harvest wind, yellow and red. But it is the trees he threshes; it is their branches that will be stored.

The dark lines of goldenness afire, shifted leftward by too much hastening away from us, reside in a region more of the red than of the yellow we have delighted in.

Of which an anecdote: We had backed further and further up the steps as the splendors before us continued. Gleaming processions passed this way and that: distantly, along the great Causeway of white marble, and further away, spiralling slowly to the top of the southern mountain, and nearby, back and forth across the columned bridges, along the ramparts rising above the shining bay. None seemed headed in the same direction. The crowds watching, like the one in which we found ourselves, seemed like the passing throngs—in white, in gold, in armor or in many-colored silks—to be filling the wide air, in a full celebration that could not quite be called gratitude. We backed further on up the steps below a statue that rose behind us, perhaps their famous chryselephantine Saturn, golden-scythed. The high sun was far from its reddened setting. But it would only be after that lowering crimson, rhymed in the red fires of the Conquerors come that same evening that, as we fled past the base of the statue, past the stone pedestal on which it rested, we should discern it indeed to have been one of Mars, sword curved in the same flat crescent as scythe, gatherer of red rather than of yellow.

Hilda laid on the gold leaf. The copy she was making of "The Miracle of the Field" flourished and sprouted under her shining care. It was not that it was a copy, nor that it was not even after some lost original. It was that it was hers. This was true plenty.

GREEN

The swallows and the early crickets with a blurred
Squeak scratched at the clear glass of the coming evening.
It was not yet dark: the surrounding green was still
Green, as if day had intended to leave a trace
Of something other than deadened gray in the black
That was to be, unmindful of the night's utter
Incapability of making remainders

Of the green into something of its own, some hushed
Nocturnal verdant. But the birds and the bugs sang
Not of this, nor of hope deepened into appalled
Silence: they chanted of nothing that was to be,
Of nothing. In the unlost green they chanted on.

In the high day, clear at the viridian noon,
Blue water, enisled in the broad grass singing hot
Choruses of summer, lies still; and far away
Half-gesturing lakes surrounded by dense, quiet
Spruces recall the silence that we are told lies
As a green hedge around blue wisdom. At the edge
Of things here and now, soft-looking cedars, waving
Away at azure, keep the sky at a distance.
If there is a leak in this green, it will have run
Into the pool, given it something of itself,
Which, rinsed in the shrillest glare of sun in water,
Will prove blue, blue derived from the wide green beyond.

And then, as if echoing all the other tones,
The noises of green thickened, and the quivering
Ground heaved gently back where it was trod upon
As if presence upon it were an entering,
Not to subvert the soft grass whose high coloring
Was that of the far heart that lay deep below them.
The tuned muscles of the earth gripped the roots around,
And yielded up unheard joy, a sobbing of mud;
Above there was a laughter of grass in delight
At the sunny loving two bright bodies contrived,
Stained with pale green, bruising the yet uncooled lawn,
 watched
Only by their own uninterested shadows.

Nomad among the verdures, you watch dark actions
Before the arras of firs, the passionless spread
Of algae only whose element throbs; pausing

In your wide amble among the phenomena
You drink the shade of the plane, and remember the
Other places of pausing, the pleasances of
Tone. Wanderer, flinging off the gauzes of day,
You too will awaken from the dust of eyesight
To the polar, the total, awaiting all with
The patience of the deep that black has when green ends,
The still unquenchable absorption of its gaze.
It will not be, can never be a mere return.

Man will nicht weiter, und man kann nicht weiter: we
Desire nothing beyond this being of green
Nor can we reach it; and even that overworked
Part of us, the eye, wearied of the vivid, stuffed
With the beneficence of leaf, seeks not to raise
Itself toward the new giddiness of heaven, clear
Though that blue may be—it would be to leave too much
Behind, the old heaviness of earth—but vaulting
The whole sequence of empurplings to alight in
Blackness, if anywhere else, in the condensed dust
Of being seen as green, turning to which darkness
Is no roving of vision, no dimming of trust.

Green: no flag of what state one is in—no peaceful
Islam widening in its cool exhalations;
No region of unreadiness; no pallor of
Young ghosts, hungry but with unbudded taste, not yet
Dyed into ripe life; no chill at body's absence;
No calmly open emblem of onward, no Go.
Stop, Traveller, here at the center of lamplight.
See how these green meanings reach even into
Unenvying meadows of mown grain, even through
Eyelike encircling blue: the green alone, unmown
As its ranked exemplars are not, buzzes with what
Is, breathes with ever-presence, with its verity.

19

(Leaves from a Roman Journal)

We who have come to this work too late, our time long past the age of missions, our own years and days turned on the road downward—we will tell ourselves, if we fail, that we were not too late, but too soon.

Instructions from the engineers to Werth: the Ponte Milvio, despite the rebuilding, may need bracing. A salvage barge would perhaps be better than working off the bridge itself; and inaccuracies in estimating the weight of the Lamp must be allowed for. But the rig suggested in the enclosed plans will probably work. Gelb is quite convinced of this, and the raising of the Lamp is, after all, his part of the project.

Krasny arrived late last night, from the far west. We met as scheduled by the dank republican temples, by a forest of tramlines; dirty, excavated only fifty years ago, somewhat overgrown, this place has never been pictorialized. Now it is awash with cats, dark below the red sunset.

Aside from the unutterable difficulty of the task itself—translating the Lamp, an Object which is somehow like a Text, across national boundaries as across a tract of time—there is the problem of all the replicas. Sagol is still not sure that all of them have been located. Sources like *Der begrabene Leuchter* (1937) are, alas, not to be trusted. Sagol is now convinced that there is something hidden in one of the old forts of the Morea, in the Peloponnesus. This will occasion a difficult overland journey if we are all to stay together. We had hoped to leave Venice by water.

One should have thought that there would be twelve of us. Two to mislead, of course; they would assist in no way with the recovery of the Lamp, but would merely fill out vacant spaces in a paradigm, would seem to be two more of us when, in fact, they would not be of *us* at all. Pomaranczowy laughed when I proposed this: "Two more to pay, two more sets of petty cash vouchers, and for nothing at all?" No, it would have been for something. The others? If there were really only ten, then, three would have had to remain unknown to the rest. Can that actually be the case now? I believe—we all believe—that we are seven. Kuan, our pilot, arrives tomorrow.

Gelb has found an old guidebook of Rome—by one Octavian Blewitt, 1850—with the well-known passage (about the Lamp having fallen into the Tiber at the same moment that the body of Maxentius was thrown off the bridge) marked in fading ink. There is a page of scrawl interleaved; I shall translate it later when there will be time.

To "find"—how peculiar a verb, so guarded in its perfective aspect. It cannot be used progressively except figuratively, with the *but . . . but . . .* of wit. Thus: "Buy this for me!" "Be patient, I am buying it"—well enough; but "Find it!" "I *am* finding it"—no he is not; his use of "find" here lies somewhere between figure of speech and that mode of lying, unmarked by the rhetoricians, of the whole for the part. Yet "find" is unrelated, after all, to "final," to endings. Its cousins are Latin bridges, Greek sea, and our own "path"; it emerged from an earlier life of sense in "to come upon." Some day when we think of these times will grammar permit us to say "We were gradually coming upon the Lamp" but not "We were finding it"?

How we are to get it out of Rome is only part of the problem, though; it has to be carried across to its home in the unimaged region, bare of representations save those of itself. Actual smaller copies of the Lamp, brass or bronze doodads as *objets de virtù* or adapted for use on minor occasions of commemoration have been expressly forbidden for centuries. Perhaps it was thus that so many images of it sprang up. The linear version of it cut in the stone at Sardis is flanked by its tender echo in nature—a frond? a leaf? a ramified trunk? Whichever, its central shaft is flanked by five linear arms on each side. A tree of eleven branches? What can it mean? Is one point missing? Is one to be disregarded? Or is it merely the inability of nature truly to signify beyond any one moment?

Questing: When there is only one task left, it is in great danger of becoming merely the image of a task. After all the great quests were done, there was the questing after new quests; but that lay outside the series and was not a part of it. We lie among the ruins of questing, here at noon on the Palatine. The grass, the sharp acanthus, the cypresses and dark umbrella pines: they guard and possess these broken stones. What kind of questing could proceed among these degrees of green? If we were embarked on a quest for the Lamp, we should surely fail: but the finding has been done. We must raise it, carry it, destroy the replicas and make restitution in the place of loss.

At the exact point of noon—at just noon—the sundial's vertical finger will be a knife edge, almost invisible. But even without the dial, we will know the moment from the grass: it will be at its greenest, remembering its early dimness when it awoke to light, invisibly dreaming its darkness to come. These are what saturate its hue, giving it depth and strength now, now.

A strangely-cut, seven-faceted stone, darker than any emerald I have seen. Werth threw it down upon the table today; it must have weighed 200 carats or more. Each of the facets, like an odd-shaped eye, surveyed us, the room, the maps, the salvage equipment. The *carabinieri* uniforms hung on a rack in the corner; the enamel paint and spraying apparatus were piled up across from them. It was as if the minimal but precise technology which had faceted the stone, had given it windows onto the world of those who watched it, stood as a kind of rebuke to our sleazy gadgetry. But what else is there to use? The nations of the earth pray to their gods with the same words and means of connecting them that are employed in telling white lies, in complaining that they have been cheated by the butcher. Our nouns are chains and hydraulic lifts, the underwater gear our tropes.

Kuan, the airman, has a theory that when the Lamp has been restored, the famous image of it here will vanish. That large, noble stone relief from oblivion—the only representation we have all had to go on—is by its very nature uncanonical. It is as if one lived by a Scripture whose original tongue had been totally forgotten, all other texts in it lost or defaced, and that had only been preserved in a mocking and contemptuous translation, elegantly but insincerely done. And yet it would have had to have done for one's Text. When I ask Kuan if the surrounding stone lictors on the relief, if Vespasian, Titus, and Domitian will vanish too, he snorts: "Those that were imaged have gone: stone may remain. When the Lamp is restored, the frail, impermanent representation will immediately wear away. All stone is as the grass, gray grass." I joke in my way, Kuan in his.

If the restoration is successful, we shall all hear of it as if a general roar had gone up in the atmosphere. If it fails, or if, the mission having been accomplished, the time is not yet ready to absorb its consequences, we shall hear nothing. Our lives will all go on as before. But the transporting will, if having been done, have been done for all time.

These are the replicas: (1) At Ferrara; the bronze one—a poor copy with no base—has been unearthed and is on its way here. It will be substituted for the Lamp and given over to the Belle Arti people as what we had dredged up, so that no Antiquity will be, as far as they know, leaving Italy. The historians were right about this one; Beatrice de Luna, living in the Veneto in the late 1540s, had it made and hidden there before she left for Constantinople. *"La Señora"*—what a legacy we have from her! (2) At Cordoba, outside the walls; this was destroyed in the attack there in July, 1936. (3) In Alexandria, lost overboard at sea when the lashings of its crate broke in a storm, 1956. (4) At Antioch, dating from the fourth century; this is to be blown up in an internecine terrorist attack. (5) And now, it appears, this last one at Karytaina. This will be my task; the others will avoid the Greek mainland after all. I shall proceed from Patras.

The interleaved notes from the old Roman guidebook: "The Pictorial Land . . . Hilda said [illegible] . . . was a meaning and purpose in each of its seven branches, and such a [illegible] cannot be lost forever. When it is found . . . as each branch [illegible] a differently colored lustre from the other six . . . shall combine into the intense white light of truth." This is all I can make out. O, the musings of tourists, moving among the ruins and the replicas!

That we should have to carry it back Eastward seems to confirm our task as one of restitution. The labors of Hercules all moved progressively Westward. There are no more heroes of the sun; ours is one labor gathered from the work of many. Just as colored lights can stain each other's field of radiance, so an imperfection in the work of any of us could impair the validity of the work of any of the others.

The great narratives are of finding and of founding. What was hidden in our case had already been found, what was to be established has been long since. Our romance is of raising and bearing, the undoing of histories. Consider: a victorious sign flew into the sky for Constantine—the antithetical Lamp to be buried tumbled off the bridge into the Tiber. It had been kept for 237 years in Vespasian's Temple of Peace. We still do not know why it was removed or by whom, on the day of Con-

’s victory. In December we shall dredge it up and take . This is almost a comic enterprise; and save for our , we are the usual comically ill-assorted lot: Krasny for security, Pomaranczowy, our paymaster and bursar, Gelb, the engineer, Werth, at the center of things, Kuan, our pilot, myself, and Sagol who navigates, plots and times. We resemble a collection of types sent up from central casting, and rejected even by Cinecittà because we looked too obvious. Perhaps in the cold light of a winter dawn, our truck snorting up the Lungotevere Flaminio, we shall look less so. But it will not matter.

Werth says that the replica in Greece is the most important one of all, the most perfect, the most false. It was in all probability the one carried to Constantinople by Belisarius. The Vandals removed many treasures from Rome to Carthage in 455. It was probably there and then that replica was made; Justinian received it as genuine in the Eastern capital and there it remained. Procopius’s fiction that it was sent back, with other valuables, to Jerusalem lest they prove unlucky for the Emperor is to be totally discounted. And so it remained in Byzantium. But for how long? I shall be spending the summer and autumn designing the removal; perhaps I can determine the history as well, even as I plan to end it.

That I am a kind of afterthought, a substitute on this mission, doesn’t bother me; that I may fail does. That I am not to participate in the raising of the Lamp from the mud doesn’t; that by some mishap I may not be there to help carry it in and over does. But it seems that wanting what is reasonable to want is itself hopeless, unreasonable and wasteful. All I have ever deserved is to be able to work at this. I shall not say “serve”—that is the language of all those nasty royal arms which proclaim indifferently *“Non Serviam”* or *“Ich Dien”*. Blazon liars. What we do is beyond serving.

At the beginning I would sit among the ruins and gaze like any pictorialist on what had been lost, and what saved—the tender sculpture of chance leaves three columns, an artfully broken piece of pediment, standing at the sentimental height midway between the composed and the sublime. I would gaze at the ruins and contemplate not reconstruction, not restoration, but restitution. What we were planning, what was being planned for us, was a serious trifling with history. Brooding over the ruins summoned up regrets: if only the barbarians' powder had been wet; if the fire had burned the other way; if the Emperor's sad, wise cousin had seized the purple . . . if, if. But this is like contemplating the ruins of one's own years. One comes to hate what was lost, but to admire the tumbled drums of column lying at provocative angles against other stones, to despise the once-finished and gleaming structure, and still to hum to oneself, droningly and incessantly, "if . . . if."

The raising itself: the date set for Sunday, November 30, at an early hour. An accident on the bridge will provide an excuse for a work crew. I shall have left the previous night, not getting to see the Lamp until we all meet again, content with a last glimpse of Werth's gleaming green stone, not standing for the thing itself, but speaking wordlessly of it. It shows a hard, cold radiance that shines outwardly through all of its ocular facets because of the excited reflections and bendings of its inner light. And thus, like all significant shapes, a picture of the attention that regards that shape as well—as what lies behind the eye perceives itself in the depths and surfaces of the smallest spill of water on a black tabletop, or in the profoundest pool set in a cup of mountain. And thus, like these, the stone is a minor text but a canonical one. It will be like, that night, a verse to speed the departure of The Last Day Before—"The earth has given its yield: may we be blessed. . . ." (A yield of green? Of stone? Of light?) I shall be driving through the dark chilling night to the south.

Karytaina. It was one of the twelve major baronies under Geoffrey de Villehardouin whose own castle lay to the south in Kalamata. The Frankish fort was built by Sir Hugh de Bruyères in 1254, sold to Andronikes II Palaiologos in 1320, taken by the Turks ca. 1460. The fort crowns the flat, rocky brow of the high town like a dull coronet, heavy and important. The replica lies under the stones of the parapet that faces southeast. The University archeological dig will have loosened the principal one, and the simplest and most silent of equipment will unearth the replica. If it cannot be destroyed on the spot, melted down right away, the helicopter will take it out with me. There is no great problem here, as the sole charge is to remove the replica from future history, soundlessly, unnoticed and without any consequences save for those that stem from the recovery of the Lamp itself.

If it were only that my parents had been poor, but had not quarreled always: it would have served. If they had battled continually, but had not used me as a broom handle: it would have served. If they had used me to brandish and bang only, but had not gone on to explain why this had to be: it would have been enough. If they had explained and expounded only, but not sent me away: it would have been enough. If they had sent me away only, but it had not been to a Home: it would have served. If I had only been sent to a Home, but had not become a model inmate: plenty. If I had become a model inmate, but the Home had not thereupon burned to the ground: it would have served. If the Home had been destroyed, but I had not in addition injured my left foot: it would have been enough. If I had only remained forever halt, but had not made a bad bargain with the crutchmaker: it would have served. If my crutch were inadequate, but I had not quested after another sort of succedaneum and prop to my infirmities: it would have been enough. If I had womanized my way into near madness only, and had not found a suitable and treacherous helpmeet: it would have sufficed. If my wife had but dug away at the Temple of My Heart only and had not taken years and years to do so: it would have sufficed. If years of hopeful peace had made the crash deafening, but I had at least been able to move from the spot: *basta!* BUT, since I could not walk away from my disasters, being stunned and rocked with grief, I saw the shadow of one stone falling across another as the day slowly breathed; I felt a nearness; I saw the task of the slowness itself of tasks. It all served. I am prepared now even for joy.

La Señora: Doña Gracia Nasi as she reconstituted herself, shedding the blessing of moonlight, journeying in the commerce of restitution from Lisbon to Amsterdam to Venice and finally to Constantinople. Perhaps it was then, at the time when her nephew and son-in-law was Duke of Naxos, that the replica was removed westward. It travelled from island to island hidden among manifest cargoes; the sailings of the summer days brought its hidden gold to Nauplion. By weeks of overland journey to the river, south of Megalopolis; by barge down the Alpheus to Karytaina, its tall head of mountain waiting at the dark high end of the long Arcadian valley. The Duke of Naxos, at the crest of his fortunes, accomplishes the queen of his acts. Why? In the knowledge that it was indeed a replica? This makes little sense. But in the prophetic modernity of not knowing, and of not daring to decree or predict? Perhaps.

I feel strangely young, as if I had acquired new qualities: the power to charm, a speaking and cheerful gaze, an aura of fragility that was somehow nonetheless being protected, and thus remaining uncoarsened by any defenses of its own. I am to embark not on a night journey, but upon a pastoral cycle of magic and simplifications. I can almost read the touchingly conventional phases of my tale. *Book I:* He drives through the night and the next day rests in Bari. *Book II:* The episode of the lady in the hotel at Brindisi. *Book III:* Terrorists attack the ferry and take the lady hostage, but dare not return to the Albanian coast. *Book IV:* The Lady escapes on Corfù; the others in Rome are notified. *Book V:* The ferry limps on to Patras; he discovers her letter. *Book VI:* Meanwhile—all has gone well in Rome; the Lamp is on its way northward. *Book VII:* Alarms in Patras; escape down the coast to Pyrgos; return north again. *Book VIII:* The lady and the producer's yacht. *Book IX:* He and she meet again on Zante. *Book X:* *"Zante, fior' di Levante";* the Old Man of the Island. *Book XI:* The vineyards of currants; narrative of the Old Man of Zante. *Book XII:* Meanwhile—the ship *Teva* out of Nicosia has sailed from Chioggia; the Lamp is on the water. *Book XIII:* The sad departure from Zante; they separate on the mainland; he meets his driver. *Book XIV:* The terrorists again: we have not seen the last of them; a narrow escape in Kyparissia. *Book XV:* Meanwhile—*Teva* in the Ionian Sea; the lady imprisoned by Customs. *Book XVI:* On the road; along the river; among the mountains; a digression on Mount Lykaion. *Book XVII:* He reaches Karytaina and confers with the archeologists; songs of the Sweet Singer of Karytaina. *Book XVIII:* Meanwhile—*Teva* off Cyprus; a storm at sea; the Lamp nearly lost overboard. *Book XIX:* Night in Karytaina; a veiled visitor at the inn: it is the lady; she reveals herself to be Fräulein Werth, the sister of our coördinator. *Book XX:* The replica; carrying it down into the valley: it is impossible to melt down; awaiting the helicopter. *Book XXI:* No news from the ship; resourcefulness of Fräulein Werth; the helicopter. *Book XXII:* The replica dropped into the sea; meanwhile—the Lamp is put safely ashore in darkness. *Book XXIII:* He and she. . . . But the last book-and-a-half of every story is always incomplete by virtue of its very closure: to finish is to leave undone the task of showing eternity, rushing out of the last event in a stream of consequences, mostly lost, like bubbles near a source. But the stream itself is all there will ever be. Now from the north the *tramontana* has come up; it blows through my pages. The umbrella pines have darkened, with evening, into the color of painted foliage under old varnish. I close the covers of my pastoral romance, dark, nubbly, green leather printed in gold, the color of the dissolving trees.

It will not go this well. Or this badly.

The Lamp has been subject only to time.

But we are now thrust into the midst of things. The summer afternoon, *romancier,* dies not with the light of the sun, but with the radiance of its own green. I think now, with the days of autumn waiting before me, of the impending grays and browns. The time of waiting is the time of rock. And my vision must narrow to the task.

I can see my moment now. Not the time of accomplishment—that instant is ever invisible, dissolved in the eddies of occurrence. I can look into the heart of the eternal first seconds of the view—from a point southeast along that Arcadian valley—of the mountain village. The sun rakes across it before sinking down behind Mount Lykaion, to the southwest; the neck of the hill embraced by the houses, the brow garlanded by the crenellated stones, the usual layers of fortification blend into the pictorial dusk: Frankish, Byzantine, Turkish. The Venetians did not touch here. My lamed eye reaches down the valley toward its dark head, whose own blind gaze commands the view toward the plain behind me. The far space and long antiquity give meaning to each other, the relation of mineral hill and ethereal sky being an encounter of very ancient presences. And yet this is an occasional vision, a wandering of the eye among accidents. It is not, say, of the long-proposed Ascent of something, planned, undertaken with a companion, glossed by a text, warned against by the rustic on the slopes, moralized on the way up and the way down, impelled in the first place by the reductively described desire to see the height—to see from, of, and toward the height—of what had always been, from the surrounding countryside of one's life, ever in view. It is not even the view toward the Pisgah from which the hedged promise of the to-be-arrived-at will gleam, to, but not for, the climber in the sunset. It is not the binocular seizure of detail, nor the important zoom into what matters for the task at hand. It is not of reaching height; it is not of squat failure. It is of the surroundingness.

BLUE

I

Day is naked even in its nuances
Of cloud: and there goes Pancho Manza, *homme*
De terre, working his own way alongside
The wide road that bandages the rye fields.

Moving along the grain, a point of shade,
He will arrive in good time to keep his
Disappointment with the dim, elusive
Horizon: stumpety-stump. Across the

Road, nightly the dark don, Freiherr of Sky,
Waits by a small pool, floating bright sequins
Over velvety water: one after
Another, they mirror diminutions

Of moon, upon which the pondering don
Reflects, his eyes lit windows of the room
Wherein crafty lamplight is at its work
On objects, and silence settles its dust.

2

At the broad border of the evening
Mercury leered out of the bold cobalt
He was returning to, remembering
Azure anterior to this night's share.

He remembered cyan: he thought again
Of high, blue air he had borne a white torch
Of morning in, of what it was to hear
The blue zones of sky torn with humming winds.

His tiny globe glowed brightly with knowing
How to tell blue from blue, where noon divides
The after from the forenight. Later, when
He knelt down among deep, waving shadows,

He smelled the exploding smalt of the sea
Fizzing away in a different kind
Of light: its hue cried out against fancy,
Against tales of its own contingency

(Such as that once a blue moon setting dipped
Deep in the broad water, dyeing it).
Above it the undying barer of
Fresh, borrowed light stared out of the blue dawn.

3

Better to say perhaps that there were two
Moons, one blue and one yellow, that green tones
Were but diseases of these, or the fruit
Of their contention at times of twilight;

And that the major illusion of moon
Was one of widening at the zenith—

Not at the seedy horizon behind
Cutout low rooftops, or second-growth woods,

The better to condense their silhouettes—
And that the creamy moonlight, spilled among
Our forms of night, fled the neutrality
Of silver kissing marble shapes in myths,

Likewise the icy light of the witch's
Eye, which drew away from like tinsellings.
Then nothing would affright the traveller
Of thicket paths: neither the yellow-made

Shade cast behind him, the Body of Bones,
Nor the blue-flung shadow of the Body
Of Work moving more slowly before him.
He would be calmed by the two modes of night.

4

But a sole moon alone hovers above
The fields of collapsed light, the acreage
Of our misfortunes, narrowed at its height;
And the hard blue line of the horizon

Divides two notional hues of ocean
Cloudy with whitecaps and of sky behind
The day's mackerel belly; it slices
Our globe of eyesight, and bluer than might

Be imagined, far more lethal than all
The bottled light of fluorescent tubes,
Unleashes the strong eager energies
Of destruction, new shatterings under

The sun, new nullifications at night.
Dawn comes when we distinguish blue from—white?
No, green—and, in agreement, eyeing the
Dying dark, our morning wariness nods.

You had best build one yourself; when bought already assembled, these things work very badly, and may leave dangerous residues.

The laser-eye is itself dangerous, for like a speaking, destroying word of light it can nullify your subjects as if they were chaoses, but leave you not alone, merely a hologram of yourself and yet accompanied still.

The control panel is located deep inside, although an unreliable terminal is available at the top, from which there is a synoptic but distorted view of the power units.

Do not make the mistake of sentimentalizing the mechanical parts: for the flywheel, archaic and precise with its gleaming spokes, is a horror of solemnity, going berserk at the insinuations of jiggle—the twin moons of the governor are a cramp on exuberance—the pistons slide easily joylessly in their cold oil—the valves twist with difficulty—the shining brass gauges were unwisely calibrated in a time of hope.

The mercury is another matter: its drops cohere so—oily but dry, like seeds of gleaming—cold sparks hinting of the tiny hot planet. It will get out of hand; yet it is absolutely essential to the working.

There can be great variation in the exterior design; one has seen many playful arrangements—some resemble machines to make or to break. But it is the circuits alone which are terrifying, and the interior spaces whose tolerances are so minute.

The energy it consumes is enormous; it is almost too expensive to operate. But of course, one must.

Those to be dealt with need not be specially prepared.

After the red alert light goes off, there will be a period of waiting; do not disintegrate them at this stage, or you too will never have existed.

Wait for the blue light to shine.

Remember that they are all despots.

If you get it to work properly, it will put an end to them, your predecessors.

DEPARTED INDIGO

My father as a boy knew her
As a gracious, kind and hooded
Lady, and her house at forty
Four hundred something Ängstrom Street
(One never needed the numbers:
It was near the end of the road)
Was open. By my day her place
Of residence was gone, its lot
Obscured by neighboring mansions.

When she dwelt among us her deep
Gaze comforted beyond smiling.
The fragile virgin of Justice
Frowned at the way things were to be
And fled, but our lost lady would
Never reign at arms' length: she loved

Her subject surfaces, but not
Those alone: a secret consort
Drank of her darkness, she of his.

Was she Madame de Violet
Or good Frau Blau? We were not told.
But where she lay she joined all hands
About her—not like the heated
Gold mediations of Venus,
Fanning the leftward yellow flames
Of her limping smith, while sharing
In the abashed reddening of
Her netted warrior rightward—

Our far lady lay among her
Saturations on either side,
Reflecting an intensity
That both possessed—the blue of day
Sky, and the violet of night—
Filling the glass pitchers of their
Transparency with a common
Pool of dark dew, from which they drank
And which suffused them with themselves.

It was for the other side of
Sunset that we needed her dark,
Connecting tone, for the richness
Of aftermath, to represent
It even to ourselves. Some said
It was so that blue be followed
By something of blue, violet
Be preceded by something of
Violet, lest they both die out;

Others felt that her realm lay just
Beyond sufficiency, making

Unacknowledged legislations
Of the rainbow, crowding her zone
Among the belts of the body
Of light: they knew this to be the
Last part of the necessary.
(What is enough? There is only
Too much, or now, in the twilight

Of abandonment, too little)
But later commentators, born
Under our poor hexarchy of
Tone may wonder how defenders
Of design can have known of her
Superfluity of hue when
It still lay among the chambers
Of color, as one of the great
Hours of Day occupies his throne.

Now, in the regions of vision
Where she dwells—not like that first frail
Maiden who fled into starlight,
A mere novel constellation,
But between these touching points of
Light—the rich, hopeful darkness seems
Deepened by her presence, under
Which we live and, hushed, still breathe the
Night air's perfume of discernment.

There are six songs, no, seven, that need to be sung in the darkness:

The Battle on the Plains, where heroes stood and fell; the Finding of the Treasure where it was hard to get to; the Founding of the Fields, where all expanded in peace; the

Dancing on the Lawns where there was nothing wrong; the Visit to the Sky, which was no wearying journey; the Farewell to the Guide, when the next stage was reached; the Darkening of It All, when it had become too late.

At first our heroes stood for us, then among us, when we stood for ourselves; now they do not even represent our sorrows. The Paul Bunyan balloon was deflated and put away when Thanksgiving had passed. Miss America farted into the microphone as if thereby to bear true witness to beauty, but that was only last season's attraction. No hero sums us up, no clown can contain us, and the Book of the People of the Book is in tatters.

So that what was lost at the end of each age was the image—not one to be discerned in water or fancied in clouds, but the image that inhered in the palpable One, letting it be at once paradigm of the Many and flesh of itself.

And so at the end of the day, the sky deepening as we walked back from the Prater, or home from the zoo, or along the river away from the fun-fair, the youngest child's balloon, the dark one, escaped from a fist tired at last, vanishing into its own element of the color between day and night.

Which the bandstand acknowledged in sweet conclusions, as horn and mellophone resolved their faintly crowded, adjacent *f* and *g* downward to *e* and *g*, firm in the faith that the ground was bearing up under them, making it seem that there had never been *f*, that thus it had ever been, healing, until the close of the soft cadence, the dominant wound.

VIOLET

At the song's beginning
Even as our voices
Rise we know the last words

And what it will sound like
To sing them at the end
Of the final burden;

Just so the cold fiddler
Hums the final chords of
Each of our capriccios

Even as he starts up.
But Jack, looking out of
The house that our song had

Him build, can see no cock
Crowing in the morn at
Break of ultimate day:

How then can we now shape
Our last stanza, furnish
This chamber of codas?

Here in the pale tan of
The yet ungathered grain
There may be time to chant

The epic of whispers
In the light of a last
Candle that may be made

To outlast its waning
Wax, a frail flame shaking
In a simulacrum

Of respiration. Oh,
We shall carry it set
Down inside a pitcher

Out into the field, late
Wonderers errant in
Among the rich flowers.

Like a star reflected
In a cup of water,
It will light up no path:

Neither will it go out.
Here at the easternmost
Edge of the sunset world

Starlings perch like quick notes
On a stave of wires high
Against the page of sky

But silently: in a
Mown oatfield what text will
The dallying night leave?

—A tree of light. A bush
Unconsumed by its fire.
Branches of flame given

Sevenfold tongue that there
Might be recompounded
Out of the smashed vessels

Of oil, of blood and stain,
Wine of grass and juice of
Violet, a final

White, here at the point of
Sky water and field all
Plunged in their own deep well

Of color whose bottom
Is all of the darkness.
If clear water is to

Give light, let it be here.
And if sound beyond breath
Of candle flame endure,

Then no wailful choir of
Natural small songs, no
Blend of winds; but let be

Heard their one undersong
Filling this vast chamber
Of continuing air

With the flickering of
Cantillation, quickened
Soon in the ringing dew.

Now, at the eastern edge of the black grass, he drinks a draught of the juice of the last flower.

Ten black drops have been flung into the night, as if by his little finger dipped into the deepest of cups;

And he considers the three higher colors that have been beyond color always; and he considers these at the dying of the wise light, remembering childhood:

In the chemist's window it was the same water that bubbled up through the differently colored glass tubes, even as oil streams forth into the lights, all the lights.

In the chemist's window, the hanging spheres of ruby, of emerald, of amber: he was told "Those are colored water" not as if a radiance had been selectively stained, but as if the colorless had been awakened from its long exile in mere transparency.

The diaspora of water ends when those colored bowls give back nothing that is untinted by their own light.

The eternities of the book end when there is only light for one eye, when the chant can be heard by only one ear: the hidden candle, the locked clavichord of implications.

Here they all were: The unfolding of What There Was
The warring of the leaves
The shaping of the rounded spore
And all that occurred therein
The opening of the codex
The echoes of wars, the shades of
 shaping
And the shadows of the echoes of
 the told told tales

They all end by the black grass, where fireflies dart about busily flickering with their hopeless fictions,

And the fiction that the first text was itself a recension of whispers, a gathering of what had been half-heard among the trees.

When morning comes, they will stop and go out, though morning will bring no light along the right-hand path on the margin of the dark.

It will be only his old man's dream of dawn that unrobes the violet, allows the early rose to take her morning dip.

He remembers this, and thinks not to quest among the regions of black for what lies beyond violet,

But would stay to hum his hymn of the hedges, where truth is one letter away from death, and will ever so be emended.

Blessed be who has crushed the olive for the oil.

Blessed be who has cracked the oil for the light.

Blessed be who has buried the light for the three tones beyond,

In which, when we have been stamped out and burned not to lie in the ashes of our dust, it will be to grow.

ON THE CALENDAR

T. 1: I will start with an ancient trumpeting in my ears, an awakening in my eyes, as if the morning of a new month were a whole new year; but as my heart cries out under the burden of these surges of hope, the great call of the trumpet, the last call of all, will crack it. As if the end of the old were the end of the whole.

W. 2: I will start a second time, awake again to an old alarm, move inevitably among the echoes of the previous day; in my family these things are always celebrated twice, and so I shall die once again of aggravated commencement.

Th. 3: I will mount a high tower of speculation, away from which the plain of the immediate world will appear to roll, not so much inaccessible as undesired. Falling—as I lean out over that flattening of past, present and future as if to inspect it more closely but for no particular reason—I will not rise to meet my maker (even my last outcry will shrink from that), but will drop toward the mud from which I was made. Only at the end of my fall that clay will be kept from me by the unopened seal of the sidewalk.

F. 4: I will eat crow, as usual, and gradually succumb to malnutrition.

S. 5: I will put my foot into that part of life from which it is impossible to withdraw it.

Su. 6: I will be holidaying in gross, comfortable Switzerland, and while walking by the lake in Geneva I will fall ill. Swiss Doctors will disagree about whether it is Tapanuli Fever or the Black Formosa Corruption, all the while I am too sick to be moved or even to protest.

M. 7: I will rise to the ocean surface after diving under a very high breaking wave, pushing all-too-slowly up into the sweet, still darkness at the bottom of too deep a well.

T. 8: I will wander into a picture gallery and this sort of thing will happen:

> "Ilion Anagrammed in Oil: Agamemnon Destroyed" will make me age vastly overnight.
>
> "The Mare of the Sea Heaves Her Vast Flanks along the Sands, or A Bad Dream of Lilith" will frighten me at night; awakening, my heart pounding, I will collapse, as I remember it, in something deeper than fear.
>
> "Silver Quickening" will emit the cold gleaming of dead metal coming to life; it will chill me.
>
> "Hewn out of the Head of Night" will turn me to stone.

W. 9: I will sit in the darkening city, my desk lamp flooding the green blotter with its own color, cancelling all my obligations, debts, vows, commitments, resolutions, one by one. I will realize only at the last instant that I have gone too far, and confessed that the implicit assertion that I am alive was, after all, a lie.

Th. 10: I will beat my breast in remorse so hard that it caves in.

F. 11: I will choke on some bones of noon hidden in my soup of the evening.

S. 12: I will discover a new continent: washed up on its beach, lying there naked and exhausted, the Princess of the Shore surrounding me with her laughing companions, I shall look up at her eyes into the smile of her father, the Lord of Hell.

Su. 13: I will enter a phase of erotic debauchery, searching among twisted regions of the Appalling for a hidden gateway into some sort of garden. Nothing will daunt me. And one calm evening of respite, I will pass into a pleasant glade of the more familiar sort of thing I had been fleeing in my explorations. Enjoying an elegantly turned-out and expensive one-legged daughter of joy, her stump tucked under my left arm for convenience in fucking, I shall succumb to a terminal transport which, given the relative absence of the uncanny, one could hardly have expected to be so strong.

M. 14: I will (a) tell a truth, (b) keep a promise and (c) dissolve away my bad faith, all incidentally and all unintentionally.

T. 15: I will enter a tabernacle in the wilderness of the city; the tabernacle, poorly built and tended, will collapse; ripe apples will drop upon my head, grapes will express themselves from bunches, falling like drops to the confused floor; a huge gray squash will crush my skull like a head.

W. 16: I will arrive at departure.

Th. 17: I will cut my finger on the sharp paper of my will while adding a new and whimsical codicil, and become infected.

F. 18: I will still be there, but everything else will have gone away.

S. 19: I will wander into a secluded part of the Central Park where three fourteen-year-olds, doubtless mistaking me for their true victim, Someone Else, will murder me for five dollars.

Su. 20: I will enter a warm, lamplit room where my father, sitting at his narrow desk over a page of log-ruled graph paper (on which the curves of increase get twisted into the lines of constancy), will look up at me and smile. His pen will be poised over the page. I will confide to him my childhood fear that he was, with sophisticated biochemical knowledge, gently and insistently poisoning me, through my food, toothpaste or mild medication. He will again reassure me, as he did in my childhood, laughing and surprised himself. And this time he will hand me, comfortingly, a poisoned drink.

M. 21: I will look in the mirror on my bedroom door and see myself from behind.

T. 22: I will write one bad line too many, it will reverse itself and, seizing the pencil from my affrighted fingers, proceed to erase all of me.

W. 23: I will join the other passengers in a slow bus as, after an eagle has flown at the windshield, causing the driver to lose control, the bus goes crashing down the lower slope of Mt. Parnassus, while other eagles wheel overhead.

Th. 24: I will take cold, finally.

F. 25: I will be three years old; I will turn a windy corner at the foot of an urban hill; an adult with a smile that I will not recognize at the time—that of a playmate with the same name as my yet unborn brother—will say "Hello!" and shoot me with a pistol.

S. 26: I will trip over a railroad tie in my dark bedroom and stub my soul.

Su. 27: I will awaken from a recurrent dream—of an unpleasant sort, but so familiar as to seem almost homely—to find myself in a low, narrow tunnel, along which I have been crawling, sharp rocks stabbing my knees and scraping my back, unable at last to move ahead or backward.

M. 28: I will issue forth, screaming, into my mother's tomb.

T. 29: I will receive from the new teller at the bank, a dim and inattentive person, a pair of strange coins made to fit perfectly over my closed eyelids; proving this by experiment, I will be hit by a large truck.

W. 30: I will attend a small party in my honor at which there will be three short girls of about seventeen, too shy to talk to me. One of them, very fat and with an almost deformedly large ass, will have so sweet and clear-skinned a face, such soft and bravely arranged hair, that my heart will break as I think of her and her isolation in and from her body. I will be found next morning in the deep snow.

Th. 31: I will pause before a shop window, long enough to see reflected in it a girl named Dot, with her name painted on her T-shirt, standing behind me awaiting recognition.

NOCTURNE

The great world turns
Cold of her own will, making stone
Of the hot heart, the rest slowly
Chilling even
Her skirts of dirt
Under which we have been mucking
About, rifling in their folds for
Flecks of gold. All of which causes
Her, enthroned in
Rock, to twitch the hem of her garb without a word.

Within the warm
Dark at the edge of the earth where
Vacancy of rock begins, we
Lie in the soft shadows of the sheets between us.
Through the windows comes the city
Light that is not
That of moon, nor yet the dark light
Of earth that will
Fall over our final length when height collapses.
It is the light in which we lie.

In the breadth of
Nightwind that shakes
The windowframes
A whisper has run out through the glass and become
The shattered lass of the courtyard,
Anna Mañana, clattering
Across shadows; round her shoulders a shawl of wind
Twitches; she sits waiting among
Dull bins and shining dark bags to
Regain a cold quondam body.

If the light lying across her
Lap makes her the Witch of Insinuation, then
We can only know her sister,
The bright Queen of Meaning, by her
Impalpability: in the clarity of
Daylight she is not to be seen,
But known by the radiance which is
Hers, giving back
What darkness keeps
Taking from us.

Call her Celia Manyhorses,
Indian giver: we remain in
Falling light, all that is left us,
Even for the eye that rises.
But this way of being unseen
Is not that of the most cloaked One:
Robed half in the glow of unbudded rose, half in
Blue too deep to read, beyond she dwells, but governs
Here and ever,
She who has arranged the marriage of dawn and death;

She whom we know by her iron
Chain, by her dry breath of what must
Be. It is she
Whom we have known all along, who prepared our dream
Of earth and breath;
She who leaves us
In the hard glare of morning with
Images out in the courtyard
Of dirt and wind,
Of what we are.

COLLECTED NOVELS

Where does one start? Perhaps here, at the middle
Of them all, as now, with *Elevenses,* that
Strange minor afterpiece, a book of partings
And mostly written on shipboard in passage
Between a new old world and an old new one,
Rocking between a fear of open ocean
And an arrival at a terror firmer
Than that, its separate sections somehow stand
For all the other novels: one can find them
There, such as in the scene where they both promise,
Standing by the inadequate lifeboat, drunk—

But you never read that one. Perhaps you did
Guess things about the juvenilia: *The*
Rock Cried Out "I'm Burning Too" was the first one
(In England called *A Universe of Death*), long,
Lyrical, assaulted by gangs of fancies,
Burdened with epigraphs, limping earnestly
Along corridors dimly lit with callow
Candor. On the other hand, *The Book of the*
Perfect Clown, the second of my first books, with
Its mock-dialogue form, inset tales, and arch
Picaro gestures, shone with counterfeit light.

Next, *My Brother's Reaper* was a mystery.
(I'd wanted its title to be *The Case of*
The Limiting Case, avowing how here the
Solution was indeed the discovery
Of the proof that the case was insoluble.)
It was an anatomy of doubt, and the
Successful but untriumphant detective
Disappeared unexplainedly at the end,
So that his career could not continue in

Other books, but only in life. Here it stands,
In all its cheap editions, with the others.

The truth is out. You have the books: I give you
Their true authorship. You'll find among them our
Collaboration, the epistolary
Most Said, about the couple who put about
Experimental rumors of their life in
Order to trace out the modellings of truth
(Keeping safe in that the facts were notional)
By friends and lovers. And about what happened to
Them thereby (we rejected *The French Letters*
As title, with "For Prevention of Disease
Only" as epigraph—but you remember . . .)

It does belong with the others—even with
That purgatorial vision, *Peeping Tom,*
Its solipsistic opposite, lonely and
Mad in its questing for certainties of light;
The intricate *récit* of an old voyeur
Epistemologist, it tells of his three
Wives, Virgilia, Matilda and Beatrice,
His three lives with them, and of his going blind
After a life of seeing wisely and far
Too well; full of long digressions on mirrors,
Cameras, pictures—not the best sort of novel.

No: the few good ones were those which went about
Their sad work of imagining marriages,
Doing what we need such texts for, providing
Models of the mysteries of pairs we are
Not part of, and mirrors of our unknown own.
Leaving, for one, and *The Right Links* and even
Merrydown, that romance of sunken heights and
Afterpleasures: broad canvases, cities and
Seaside sojourns, many households, and, that there

Be truth, humming swarms of irrelevancies—
These redeemed the early games and drawn-out songs.

The novel of wartime London, *Dark Cremorne,*
Hardly a failure, dwelt in its retractions
Of vision—squinting through magnesium glare,
Turning emptied eyes toward the cold dawn—and was
One with its minima—few characters, a
Minor rondo of fewer locales, even
The poor, grey wartime paper of the book James
Chamberlain was reading, sad food, those frightful
Knickers to be got past to delicate hairs.
Yet these simple, enviable pleasures robbed
From death seem bright idylls of denial now.

(No, *Blackbird Cross* would have been a bad title
—Taken from the bus-route terminus and, of
Course, from Helen Elizabeth's dream: you must
Have guessed by now what part you played in it.) But
About the destroyed manuscripts of what was
To have been *Jealousy* I shall say nothing.
It is not here among the works. It might have
Been the worst or the best—a vivisection
Of desperate knowledges and narrowings,
Of the sense that one's death is being kept from
One—or one's life. The earliest drafts were endless.

They are finally together on the shelf—
As if about to be packed up for moving—
Here at a somber time of dissolution,
Leaning wearily against each other: some
From out of the closet and still dusty with
Concealment, some that had been staring out at
You all along, others from scattered regions
Of the house, huddling together, refugees
Bereft if not of their titles then of their

Various makers' names—the ones in which I
Penned them (or in which I, too, was penned). All mine.

Having no terror of design, you would not
Have dreaded knowing that all these works had one
Author. But that I failed to write them under
My true name is not a matter merely for
The spirit's connoisseurship: to gather them
Here, half a dusty sheaf of hybrid grains, is
To acknowledge the too early arrival
Of frost, the race for a few last hours of light
To read by, to plant or reap by. I would have
Given you their common life: I have left you
Them, though, like eleven expired leases:

The last one, in press, being *Some Natural
Tears,* which we were to have read together, hand
In hand. You may perhaps now guess its subject—
The old story we all know and can never
Comprehend, its fierce transfers of elation
Across the bound of loss, its presentiments
Of endings, departures in the evening
Shade of sky and distant horizontal woods.
Announced in this reprint of *Elevenses,*
It shall at least reach you under my own name.

THE LADY OF THE CASTLE

Venus Pudica stands, bent. Where her hand is
Cupping her marble mound a mystery has
Come into being as the sculptor hides what
    Stone could not show yet,

Nor bronze expound. The goddess may be guarding
Herself, or in a special mode of pointing
Out (should we call it "curving in"?) her temple,
    Teaching her children

The central and precious, where they may be found.
Or indeed, as the girls say, she is hiding
Nothing, nor instructing—she is caressing
    That which she barely

Touches, warming those feelings which for her are
Wisdom blossoming even within marble.
What her maker buried she loves, and thereby
    We are revealed it.

Far in the minimal North, some contracted
Hand or eye has carved into senseless clunch an
Impudent and schematic presence, done in
    Primal intaglio,

A circle head perched on a larger circle
Of lady body, spidery legs drawn up
And outward showing off on the church tower
    Under the clock, and

Cut in a sort of Linear C, her slit.
Her hands touch nothing but her knees held open.
It is not she who joys in it, nor teaches;
    But from beneath her

55

A very well-hung personage indeed is
Climbing up toward her, as if far from having
Merely no words for things, their sculptor had no
        Method of using

Images for them: no things, only actions.
And thus translated into language her wedge
Would be a "Let's-get-up-on-her-and-in-there."
        Hieroglyphic

Of nature's own cuneiform, she sits high
But almost hiding in the irrelevance
Of a religious building now to the young
        Mums of the village.

Ignored, then, or misread by mythographers
—Myopically concluding that a corpus
Christi lies beneath a bungled cross—as a
        Crude Deposition,

She with her terrible thin cut is not to
Be any the less feared by those who read signs
And remember instances of their wide truths
        Narrowed in darkness:

Hers is the closed door into the stone again.
The soft traps having long since sprung, the marble
Self-adoring dolls long crumbled, hers is the
        Linear kingdom.

THE ANGLER'S STORY

I let down my long line; it went falling; I pulled. Up came
A bucket of bad sleep in which tongues were sloshing about
Like frogs and dark fish, breaking the surface of silence, the
Forgetfulness, with what would have been brightness in any
Other element, flash of wave, residual bubbling,
But were here belches of shadow churned up by the jostling
Tongues from the imageless thick bottom of the heavy pail.
I could not reach into that fell stuff after them, nor fling
Them back into night like inadequate fish; nor would they
Lie flat and silent like sogged leaves that had been flung under
Mud, but burbled of language too heavy to be borne, of
Drowned inflections and smashed predications, exactness pulped
Into an ooze of the mere desire to utter. It was
My bucket, and I have had to continue to listen.

HERE IS THE SUN: THE SUMMER AFTERNOON IS HOT WITH WASPS

Here is the philosopher and here is the banana.
Can the fat, yellow finger unable to grasp a hand
That plucks it, let alone a point, consume such attention?
The philosopher can eat the banana but the meal
Would be devoid of significance: not for bananas
Being the comical fruit (whoever peels one becomes
A monkey momentarily; and how could our old Loss
Of Perfection and our just recompense of What There Is
Have depended upon the imperatives of such a
Funny bunch, hanging accessibly above our first heads?)
Here they are. One will rot without wondering,
"Is a horse slipping on a banana peel not funny?"
Without regarding, in the shadow of the banana,
The fruit of the joke. Time is the ape of the absolute.

AFTER AN OLD TEXT

His head is in the heavens, who across the
Narrow canyon of pillow from yours harkens
With gazing hand and hearing knees through darkness,
    Looking and listening

To the sweet quietude of terminating
Conversation, the gentle brief wake for the
Long-dead day, the keening of his shortened
    Breath on your shoulder:

This revision of you sucks out the sound of
Words from my mouth, my tongue collapses, my legs
Flag, my ears roar, my eyes are blind with flame; my
    Head is in hell then.

LOOKING EAST ON TWELFTH STREET

On an afternoon "of extraordinary splendour and beauty"
The late, blue sky pours into the jagged mold
Of buildings racing down the street toward a vanishing point.
Houses are bright above and reassuringly shadowed
Below, and "clarity" no longer needs to mean
Unfuzziness, as it does, but regains its old sense
Of famous brightness; so that the view straight across town,
Lit by a sun who has skipped back behind one to see
His work from a distance, is a look into something inside
A theatrical preparation like the holes
Cut into the back of the world at Palladio's
Theatre in Vicenza. But it is for the solitary
Rambler of avenues to read in passing, this illustration
On a turning page of a passage from earlier
In the book when there were to have been two figures
Receding down the sidewalk to join the shaded
Part of the scene. Their walking would have been joyful, their
Disappearance at the end a sign that they had been welcomed.
The perspective is correct only for a moment
Of walking by, for the eye that aims north of that scrapes
The cracked sidewalks below with the wet point of its gaze.

From Tales Told of the Fathers

THE HEAD OF THE BED

for Robert Penn Warren

At the mountainous border of our two countries there is a village; it stands just below a pass, but some of the older houses lie higher up along the road, overlooking more of the valley than one might think. The border has never been heavily guarded, and our countries are peaceful. Theirs lies beyond the pass; in the other valley a large village looks up toward the mountains and toward us. The border itself is marked only by an occasional sign; but then there is the Trumpeter. His clear, triadic melodies break out through the frosty air, or through the swirling mists. From below, from above, the sound is commandingly clear, and it seems to divide the air as the border divides the land. It can be heard at no fixed intervals, and yet with a regularity which we accept, but cannot calculate. No one knows whether the Trumpeter is theirs or ours.

I

Heard through lids slammed down over darkened glass,
Trees shift in their tattered sheets, tossing in
Shallow sleep underneath the snoring wind.

A dream of forests far inside such sleep
As wakeful birds perched high in a dread wood,
Brooding over torn leaves, might mutter of

Rises over the pain of a snapped twig
That ebbs and throbs not with a shore rhythm
But with the pulsings of dark groves—as if

A bird of hurting swept over hooded
Places, fled, and at intervals returned—
Clocked by the broken aspirates roaring

Along their own wind, heard within their wood,
Their own deep wood, where, fluttering, first words
Emerge, wrapped in slowly unfolding leaves.

2

Where, where, where? Where is here? Where is Herr Haar,
Tendrils lashing across the light his eyes
Open on, Joker of Awakening?

Where is where? Where the cracked suddenness wide
On that frail wall, where amber filigree
As of an egg's marble vein his pillow;

Where webby vines clinging coldly to his
White eyeball fall away to dust; where hair
Hangs across the world, here is where. And there

Is the acknowledging skull of far wall—
Two hollow, shaded windows and a smudge
Of dark mirror between. And there is here

No light. Not yet. Deep in the woods' heart, soft,
Dim leaves close up again; heat lightning rips
Pallid sheets, silent, across roughened sky.

3

Floor lamps and their shadows warmed the room where
He lay dead in bed; and then the windows
Were thrown open to admit of the night.

Exhalations of buses rose hoarsely
Over the reservoir's onyx water
Beaded about with lights, an appalling

Brooch clutching the appalling shawl of the
Dark park through whose trees no relieving wind
Blew. No zephyr sniffed the window curtains

Pushing through the stuff of outer silence
That cars coughed in; only an old great-aunt
Waited, on her nightly visitation,

Denied again by his awakened, dark
Blood, as come bubbling up bone-gathering
Trumpetings of unscheduled, sombre cocks.

4

Slanting, lean, gray rain washing the palace
Steps floods the inner court: Vashti mutters
There, dripping among her ancillaries,

Of displeasure, loss, and now a cold walk
To distant parts of the palace, gutters
Roaring with possibilities, water

Burbling the Ballade of All the Dark Queens—
Not the wet abjects, but those who yet reign
(*Where is Lilith?*) in that they could refrain—

Not Hagar sent out among the dry rocks,
But Orpah opting for hers, and Martha
Answering her own hearth and electing

The bubbling merriment of her pudding,
Reading the night-girl Lilith's name in white,
Vanishing from her windy, drying sheets.

5

Coarse breath fanning the closed air by his ear
Stirred up the swarming night-bees who had been
Honeying nearby, where faces blossomed

Out of the darkness, where creepers mingled
With long, low-lying trunks, humming among
Damp hollows, herding and gathering there,

But unheard by him undreaming, by him
Beamed in upon by the wide moon who smeared
Light here and there into dark surfaces—

Madam Cataplasma, her anointment
Vast, her own outstretched form fantastic there
Beside him, as if on awakening

A filthy myth of Lilith would lie spilled
Like darkness on the sheet of light. He rolled
Out of this bad glade and slept darkly on.

6

He felt his hand feeling another hand
Feeling his own: staring up after a
Fly's noisiness, his bony image lay

Where he was beside himself, imbedded
In the nearby, the space readied and wide
And yawning, fed up with the emptiness

Of its tents, rags of cloudy percale hung
Over bumps and hummocks. It shaded them,
He and he lying and listening while

Kicked fabric fell softly over their bones.
Sighing settles: toward what does buzzing fly?
About what does the sound of breathing dream?—

An echo fleeing down twisted halls; a
Buzzing fly rising over him and his
Like something bland and vague deserting them.

7

Down the shaded street, toward an avenue
Of light, a gleaming picture receded:
The sudden lady, tall, fair and distant

Glided slowly, and her beautiful leg
Sole but unlonely, swung walking along
Between the companionable crutches,

Flesh hand in hand with sticks. He followed them
And waited in a sunny place, and when
She halted, there were woods. Turning her head,

She smiled a bad smile, framed by a shadow
Flung from a tower somewhere. He dared not move
Toward her one leg, toward her covered places

Lest he be lost at once, staring at where
Lay, bared in the hardened moonlight, a stump
Pearly and smooth, a tuft of forest grass.

8

The Hyperboreans gathered him up
And bore him across, out of the shadows,
Into their realm of tenderness where there

Is room enough, but where there are no gaps
Between the seeding and the gathering;
Nor wintering, in which recovering

Desire grows in its caves, nor the buzz
Of endless August, golden, deified:
No need for these. In that bland land he lay—

Envisioning frost and fallen silver,
Half hearing the cricket in the parching
Oat-straw, feeling tears from his weeping brow,

Dreaming of intervals lost—stretched out on
Wastes not of snow, nor sand, nor cloud, he tossed,
And knew not why, in that undying noon.

9

Leaving that unfair, seasonless land was
More than a traverse of uneasiness;
More than an antlike file over glacial

Sheets and then, at last, across the fold of
Pass, pausing above a final valley
Shining in a new light, and shivering

At the approach of strange, dark guards; more than
Their distrust, and their icy moustaches
Masking frowns at our tokens of passage

(He held a light bulb, heavy in his right
Pocket, and they, red stones in their left ones)
More than making one's way; and returning

Over a way not yet gone over, hurt
Like first smashings of light, shrunk to a lamp
Shaded, grim, sun-colored at four A.M.

10

Beyond the cold, blue mountain and beyond
That, we shall wander on the pale hills when
Shadows give over bending along the

Slopes, and the silent midday light, unchanged
For hours and days, is pierced only by our
Two moving specks, only by the cricket's

Warm humming. Then, what we hear becoming
What we see, the gray; the wind enclosing;
The poplars' breath; the sad, waiting chambers.

Will there have been room? There will have been room
To come upon the end of summer where
Clustered, blue grapes hang in a shattered bell,

Or there, in a far, distant field, a swarm
Of bees in a helmet, metal yielding
Honey, balmy drops glistening on bronze.

11

Half his days he had passed in the shadow
Of the earth: not the cold, grassy shade cast
By a pale of cypresses, by pines spread

More softly across stony hilltops; not
Warm, gray veiling of sunlight that blotted
Up his own moving shadow on the ground;

But the dark cloak of substance beyond mass,
Though heavy, flung with diurnal panache
Over his heavier head, weighed it down.

Way down at the bottom of a shaft sunk
Through the grass of sleep to deep stone he lay,
Draped in the shade cast inward by the place

All outward shadows fall upon, and on
His tongue an emerald glittered, unseen,
A green stone colder in the mouth than glass.

12

When, as if late some night of festival
The skies open, do the insides of stars
Turn slowly out? At midnight, once, he finds

Himself looking up a familiar
Street and being shown a way of water:
Bordering the calm, unsubsided flood,

Gray frame houses with darkened roofs intact,
Minding the sky of paler gray; along
The surface of gray water, the tracing

Eye's anxious questions—only these have moved.
And save where—by a window giving on
His sunken yard—someone blind makes wordless

Music while his three graceless daughters wait
In the shadows for evening, all is gray
Silence, save for his resolved organ chords.

13

He awoke. Low in the sky in August
Blown clear by a cold wind, thinned-out clusters
Of distant stars whistling through darkness struck

69

Out at a momentary Jupiter
Passing at night, bright visitor, among
The passages of his twinkling bazaars.

And saw strung in the Scorpion a jewel
Of unmarred garnet, the old, the reddened
But not with shed blood, nor with ripening.

And saw and read by the diamonded Harp,
By crossbow Swan aimed along the pale stream
Southward, by all the miles of undialled light,

By the mark missed, by the unstinging tail,
The moment that was: the time of this dark
Light beyond, that seemed to be light above.

14

Grayish flakes like clay are falling as if
Of the sky falling at last on Chicken
Big, now grown huge and old, examining

The falling daylight from her crowded house,
The plausible, settled-for gray, dropping
Out of its cloudy, indeterminate

Swirl, its pale precipitate vanishing
At the full bottom of its fall, too light
To have swerved, too general to pile up,

These flakes of day, in a reaction
As if of flakes of, say, fictions taking
Place *in vitro,* trembling as the flask shakes—

In vivo then? behind this mottled glass
The awakener hears the greasy rain
Collapse on unglistening streets below.

15

The bright moon offends him: he plucks it out;
He opens all the seals of touch; he hears
The whirlwinds of his breathing; then it comes:

A last waking to a trumpet of light
From warm lamps turns him over gravely toward
Her long, bare figure, Lady Evening,

Who, while he lay unwaking, rearranged
Oddments of day on a dressing table,
Lowered gentle blinds, letting the night dawn,

And thought of their sole parting, the breaking
Of day; his journeys into day's mock night;
His sojourn with lilting Miss Noctae, witch

Of windless darknesses; his presiding
Eye, and his slowly unwinding heart;
Then lay beside him as the lamps burned on.

THE SHADES

I

Even the white shade could flap a black wing
As it flew and wrapped itself up, clearing
Stark panes of upper window—glassy light
Slapped his eye from a sudden firmament.
When lowered, they yielded up pale shades thrown
By an inner light past the opaque ones
They were ghosts of—the pallor of the shades
Took more toll of his waking eye than dark.
And, when drawn, black ones made the scene they framed
Squint, his large light-gathering glass ducking
Below the edge where the flat night machine
Widened the strip of wall, bed, and undressed
Flesh into a picture. And his eyes were opened,
As in blinding light the hand's shade allows.

2

"In enigma, the eyes hide their own light
Behind owl eyes of darkling glass; we find
Dull scales hardening on vision's surface
As if the unskeptical patient hoped
Somehow to chain down the beasts of wild glare,
The lions of the light. The prognosis
Is neither here nor there," the Ophthalmage
Muttered over his speculum, tapping
On the onyx tabletop, which glistened
To him unhearing, being too wild-eyed
In the way of dark spectacles which fail
To widen the openings they cover,
Two tiny bullet holes known to be too
Narrow, punched through the yielding skin of mind.

3

Feeling their dark ones to have been darkened
By the cast shadows of men full on men,
They considered how the unsounded caves
Everywhere glistened; how in the silence
Of noon, there in the square, all the lighted
Sepulchres threw no shadows about them
Nor none within; how they were all faded
Angels of each other, met outside a
Garden's walls whereon their own shadows fell,
Within which walked the clear, transparent ones,
The pair of glass, whose shadows permitted
—Everything was permitted—light outlined
By their shining-edged forms to pass back up
To clear eyes from the green, mirroring grass.

4

Black Wolfgang and gray brother Ludwig, two
Shades of cat, pussyfoot down the long hall.
All the Crayola boys in flowery
Surplices sing out of their stalls in praise
Of paling and of darkening, the light
Diastole, the heavier return,
Joy being in their dance of contrasts, life
Hanging between earthwardness and the air.
Too much of too many colors brings mud,
Touches of pale water lead to lightness,
But all gathered by the eyes' firelight,
Whose very flickerings discern themselves
To be waltzing in the masquerade of
Degree, each denser he whirling off with
Her, his frail one, darkening in his arms.

5

Never having, like orange monarchs, claimed
Bright meadows rich with daylong, green milkweed,
Or flamed amazement over a gazer,
They mottle the walls of hell; they stand in
Fives in the unreturning *traghetto*
Or wrapped up in shades of death accosting
The fancy wanderers in their tunnel;
Unprimed for darkness cast on their eyelight
Itself, these find no shadows of shades here,
No shadows more than shadows of flesh, no
Flickering images of soul, no soul—
The body's pale nightmare of mind, faded;
The mind's drop of frightened sweat at mere thought
Of body, unglistening, chilled and dried.

6

With the light ever going, they live with
No walker in the cool of the evening,
Acknowledging light under chestnut leaves
In solemn motley genuinely flecked;
Uncheckered their dale, their evening no flung
Counterpane nor dark-knitted comforter,
Even, under which they crowd with their own
Heats and lights still clutched and minded; feeling
The first chill of autumn only in sleep,
They awaken to yellow sun ducking
Low under the shades to stretch trapezoids
Over a dark floor. And they sleep unminding
The time of afternoon, nearly before
The cold fading unrolled along the grass.

TALES TOLD OF THE FATHERS

1 THE MOMENT

In a cold glade sacred to nothing
He stood waiting, withholding his gaze
From unquestioned sky, unanswering
Grass, he later supposed, all the while
Growing unfelt beneath his bared soles.
The sky was not green although the grass
Was gray, and he felt the moment pass,
With no breath, when some ten of them might
Have come whispering through the dark brush,
Past spaces of water and beyond
Regions of erased shapes in the air,
To conduct him far away on foot
To a place not of earth, but only
Of abominations: dirt and soil,
Shit and mud mingling in wet trenches,
Where he would have stood bound and retching,
Aghast, but of course unsurprised as
Soundlessly the things were done, as then
The trembling foal dropped into a vat
Of rotten wine, the kid fell forward
Into the seething milk—but the wind
Breathed for him; the moment came and went
For the thin ten that time. He would wait.

2 THE PICTURES

His reflection in water said:
The father is light's general,
The son is but a morning star
Whose very rising into the
Failure of daylight makes the great
Case of upward fall—O see him
Bleaching out in the high morning!

His cold shadow on the rock said:
Under me, unshading, lies the
Skeleton of an Indian.
The dead. The dead are not even
Things. No odd beings. Stones and bones
Fall away to bone and stone then
To crumbling, then to part of night.

3 A CUP OF TREMBLINGS

Facing deep wine raised in the
Tilted, earthen cup, the dark
Opening into further
Dark, eyes wide, he could perceive,
Around the rim of the dark,
Breathings of the afternoon;
As, eyes shuttered, he could see
Sleep, so, opened, they would show
Him death—but now momently
In the heart of the wine, far
Away, the muses of waltz
Moved, as if seen from a height
Down a narrowing defile,
In an unshadowed meadow.

4 THE SIGN

When he saw a skull floating
On the face of the waters
With a mind of air and eyes
Of wind, it was not a sign
Of drowning generations
Themselves now drowned. It was no
Mere wonder of mirroring,
But part of the garbage of
Pain, the usual offal

Of encounter: a fallen
Top of something no choiring
Winds' melismata question,
The dark, hollow shard of a
Vessel of decreated
Clay, a cup of life emptied.

—And seeing it just at noon,
Bobbing on bright water at
The most transparent time, when
He could look back over his
Shoulder and see a clear field,
When his long, ever-vengeful
Shadow vanishes and stops,
For a moment, following:
This was most dreadful of all.

5 THE GARDEN

High on his brick cliff his garden hung
Open eastward and backed against the
Heights that hid the broad, showy deathbed
Of the sun, whose Tiepolo gestures
He read raving reviews of in the
Fiery mirrors of the west-watching
Windows set in other distant cliffs.
It was there that he muttered about
His pots of spiky dill and broad mint,
His borders of concealing privet.
Edenist of the mid-air, he gazed
At the black oily kernels of dust
Flung as if by some high sower and
Languidly fallen through the forenoon
Over the walls, mingling with his soil.
He had had to make do among smut
And fruitless grit; had lopped and pruned all

The branches of shadow and with care
Hung the leathern mock-adder among
His greens to scare grumbling doves away.
In the evening cool his dull cigar
Breathed and glowed. This was all that there was
To keep. And there was nothing to lose.

BEING ALONE IN THE FIELD

What had I fallen to? Even the field
Felt higher than I, the ghosts of its oats
Waving invisibly in the purple
Air above me and the height of my eye.

The sight of my eye lowered toward rising
Ground, the light of my sigh sown there, the cry
Of blood rising toward the spirits of wheat
Rusting their high ears, the listening dew

—All had composed themselves in the field, where
The darker air had flown and alighted,
And there was no light by which I might read
The field, much less as I had always done

Make it out through the Book of the Fair Field,
Or some such book. There was surely no light
For that. The absorbing bare field alone
Lay open like a blind eye turned upward.

I lay flat thus against the horizon
Which drew in towards the ground, as the flat night
Prepared in all directions save for that
Of height its draped, illegible deathbed.

ROTATION OF CROPS

Farmer John wandered among his fields
Feeling a tedium of the soil
Lifted by no pious following
Of oats by peas, then of peas by beans,
And then beans by orient barley,
Or even the peaceful fallowness
Yielding what little that peace can yield.
No dew pearled rough furrows with early
Seeds of shining along their low sills.

What could revolve there was not the sun.
Twilight kept shifting between evils
—Heaviness, then alleviation;
Only Sol smoldered with tedium
In the untenanted meads above,
There, where no other kinds of light grazed.
Below, no other kinds of light grew.
"And so, and so" groaned the Farmer John
And gazed at the vagueness of his grain.

But then after dark the night itself
Shifted her ground: cerements of turf
Flung back the rough darkness threshed away
From fire toward the stars' clear counterpane;
Hectares of millet, disgusting fields
Of vetch, acres of darkened corn, were
Turning in the starlight that seeded
Them all, while the sleeping Farmer gleaned
Mindfulls from outside the mills of light.

THE ZIZ

What is the Ziz?
                    It is not quite
Written how at the Beginning,
Along with the Behemoth of
Earth and the deep Leviathan,
A third was set forth (as if air
Could share a viceroy with fire,
A third only): This is the Ziz.

The Rabbi Aquila then asked:

Can we thrall him and his entailed
Space in our glance? And can we cast
A look wide enough to draw up
A glimpse of fluttering over
The chimney-stacks, of flashing in
Huge fir-boughs, or among high crags
Sinking at dusk? How could we have
Lime or twigs or patience enough
To snare the Ziz? The Phoenix lives
Blessedly in belts of hidden
Fire, guarding us from the hurt of
Light beyond sunlight: but where is
The Ziz? A gleaming, transparent
Class, kingdom of all the winged?
Pre-existing its instances,
It covers them, it covers us
With no shadow that we can see:
But the dark of its wings tinges
What flutters in the shadows' heart.

Even more, Rabbi Jonah said:

In their last whispered syllables
The muffled whatziz, the shrouded
Whooziz (trailing a sorrowful
Feather from beneath its cloak) tell
False tales of the Ziz: his is not

Theirs, nor he their wintry answer.
—Nor should we desire August light,
Showing a prematurely full
Sight of the Ziz entire, lest we
See and see and see our eyes out:
No: Praised be the cool, textual
Hearsay by which we beware the
Unvarying stare of the Ziz
In whose gaze curiosity
Rusts, and all quests are suspended.

At which Ben-Tarnegol recalled:

One day at the end of days, the
General Grand Collation will
Feature the deliciously
Prepared Ziz, fragrant far beyond
Spiciness, dazzling far beyond
The poor, bland sweetness of our meals;
Faster than feasting, eternal
Past the range of our enoughness:
So, promised in time, the future
Repast; but now, only vastness
We are blind to, a birdhood
To cover the head of the sky.

COHEN ON THE TELEPHONE

Hello? Something wrong again? O hell!
—Rather darkness audible, abuzz
With nasty wings small enough to whirr
Electrically in a forest
Of noises through which no darkling bird
Squawks its response to darkness, or shrills
Its orisons toward the edge of light.
No lost or dropped angels wander here:
The ghosts of noise are only of noise.

Telephones? Well, a sage said, *they can*
Teach that what we say Here is heard There.
But, grinding away at homely bells,
We can no longer talk to Central;
The Exchanges are unmanned; the poles
Are blown down; your three minutes are up.

Instruments? They are deaf: yea, the sweet
Harp of the psalmist could never hear
Its own early arpeggios rising.
The distant ringing is not the sound
Of another's bell reduced to dry
Gasps: it is produced against your ear.
It is not Levi on the Muzak,
Fiddling tonelessly with the bright dials.
It is Ben Cole, the son of your voice,
Questioning along the deep cables,
Sad and nasal even in his yeas.

And once connected to chaos, then
What engulfs you is the babbling of
The multitude of your descendants
Who clamor for a hearing now, not
Then, begetting echoes of themselves

Even as they swarm in the light wind
That blows among jungles of wiring:
Come, come they sang, but *Abbadabba*
Now they sing; until, as if you heard
The planet's end, they are clicked away.
No dial-tone, like a patient front door
May yet open on fields of people,
Bright fields. There is no waiting for dark,
Nor will the long silence break with light.
But from near, from far, unechoing
In the black sea shell you, landsman, hold
Close against your ear, it comes, it comes:

The next voice you hear will be your own.

GIVEN WITH A GOLD CHAIN

Clasping, yet unchained
To what it holds, a hand
Giving of gold may take
Thereby yet something golden.
Chains of iron enforce
Dark bondages, then may break;
Silver dims and wanes;
Brass is brass of course;
And though there was only one
Golden chain once, upon
Which everything depended,
Yours, this common one, bright
But somehow humanely reddened,
Its links remaining right,
Is finite but unended:
Too narrow, like all our circles,
To seem an eternal one,

A serious, fallen chain
Like one of shells or berries
Hung in the gentle arc
Of homely catenaries
Our bodies make—not stark
Parabolas of pain—
When crumpled out of shape
And fallen out of glitter
Into a handful of gold
Chinkingly, will mutter
Still of its olden meaning:
"Ever is my end
Consumed in my beginning"
Nothing can ascend
A frail, ungraded chain
Looped, or bunched however,
No Dark Form undertake
To give it an adverse shake
In certainty or doubt.
As you rush into the year
Of life I hurtle out of
I hand you, without fear
That nothing can be maintained,
Gold, like the touch of hands
Clasping, but unchained.

AFTER CALLIMACHUS

Half my soul still breathes;
Half, breathless, flutters
About in the dark
In love or running
Wild among others,
Gone over the hill.

Deserters get shot:
Help me find her; she
Is out there somewhere
Now, one of those flakes
Of white on the waves
Which play with her as
With my straining eyes.

A SEASON IN HELLAS

You know a region higher than these crags?
A painted castle flying silly flags
Imprisons a spoiled princess, robed in fur,
Daily awaiting a dark torturer.
You know the place? O there, O there,
On fire, O my destroyer, we shall fare!

You know the valley where a thinning stream
Reflects no hopeful spires, no peaks of dream?
A ruined roadway winds down from the pass
Toward sullen sheep, gray in the withering grass,
You know the place? O there, O there,
At dawn, O my deserter, I shall stare!

You know the bed in a long-windowed room?
Night-colored curtains stir, black roses bloom;
Where moonlit harpstrings glitter like a crown
My silvery double enters and lies down.
You know the place? O there, O there,
O my lost self, we both dissolve in air!

MOUNT BLANK

for David Kalstone

Accessible by reasonably good roads most of the year; pass open from the North, July & August. At 1973m. a rest-house, from which one can walk, or ride by cable car, to the western summit. The eastern face should not be attempted without a guide.

——Until, the next morning in the sun, there
It was, framed in the window, looking like
The intense pictures of itself, which all
The night before while the ravening black
Swallowed the hills, engorged the dim vales, sucked
Up starlight through holes in the pines, and coughed
At the half-latched gate, all the night before
He lay awake, trying to remember:
Snowy veils of spume blown across the gorge;
A view shot upward dizzyingly while
The unseen ravine somehow made itself
Known, out of the picture; even the mere
Gorgeousness of depth, rock and height had dimmed.
His cold remembrances raved in the dark,
Houring after images. Midnight
Was no minimum, though: no skier whizzed
Past its momentary flatness, down one
Half parabolic dream of slope and up
Its opposite. The deadly hours which
Followed neither sank nor rose toward the day,
But merely stretched. The pictures were all wrong,
Those which came. They were pictures of pictures,
Or views of noise: postcards of roaring, as
Of mighty waters from the top of Mount
Throwdown; illuminations of the blasts
Hammering the clear tops of Mount Windows.

Or else they mirrored certain infamous
Peaks, quite as if to lead him by the head
To some mad eminence—say, the summit
Of Nayvel, to howl a loud howl like, "Down,
Be thou my Up." Or else they reflected
The ludicrous Snifflehorn rising from
His flat face on the plain bed, pictures far
Too close to themselves, and too close to him.

No, there were to be no comparisons—
Nor of the splended reals of the morning
With night's thin images, nor of the blaze
Of day with what lay banked in a black stove,
Nor of the pictured with the picturing.
For he awoke to a deluge of light,
And, rising far beyond that light in which
His eyesight gleamed, the old and the famous
Peak, preposterous—that was what he faced.
And if it had been cut out of cardboard,
Cardboard would serve. It always had: inside
Contours part jagged, part caressingly
Smooth—for even children were trained to trace
Its silhouette that they might come to know
It—there was only the unmarked flatness
Of surface fused to its depth. What he saw
Was not a picture of his seeing, nor
An image of his dimmest sleep. And, say,
That there was no cardboard (or, if there were,
A little azure hat for the mountain,
Doing no harm), say that the crookedness
Of its high tower was a beckoning,
And that it was a place to get to—still,
Cardboard is as cardboard does: biting out
Its parts of the available blue and
Masking some gummier construction taped
Behind it, emptiness and passe-partout.

And yet the vision of it hung there seemed
A vision as of something rounded, cut
Into by the wild blades of icy air,
Scooped and shaped if only by its shadows,
Troughed by a glacier and likely as not
Hacked out with caves and rock-studded across
An unseen face. And he knew a cold wind,
Then. It brought with it, as it might carry
A distant shouting among its own yells,
A blast of glimpsing from afar, a speck
Of mountaineer against the blue, plunging
Slowly from the far summit. Then the wind
Died. Frost on the glass outside gleamed under
The mounting sun, the cold snowfields stretching
Between his crying eye and that height, the
Fell beacon, gray, unsurmounted with light.

BREADTH. CIRCLE. DESERT. MONARCH. MONTH. WISDOM. (for which there are no rhymes)

Not as *height* rises into lightness
Nor as *length* strengthens—say, the accepting eye
Calmed by a longing of shoreline—
Breadth wields its increase over nothing, to the greater
Glory of nothing: our unwanted dimension,
Yet necessary.

What the *square* can share of its rightness
Extends a just plainness; the sure swerve of a
Curve continues beyond itself.
But O, the old closure! *Circle* of will returning
Inward to prison, wrenching all tangencies back,
Lest there be friendship

Even in clever touchings that the
City solders with pity or with desiring,
Or of *mountain's* unique bond with
The fountains gushing forth from it that cry out of high
Things. Solitariness of *Desert* ever
Stretches out in vain,

Lonely *Monarch* of all who survey
Its wearying inclusiveness, subject to
No true attachments as a *fool's*
To his toy tool, jingling self-image, nor object of
Blunderings that it keeps ever breeding—*wife* of
Self-created strife.

Sole rondures of *day* unrolling stay
The approach of stillness, and between them and
The larger wheel of *year* appear
The lunar counterturns in cold, reflected selfhood
Of *Month,* unbound to sun but only barely out
Of phase with its rounds.

These solitaries! whether bright or
Dim, unconstellated words rain down through the
Darkness: after *youth* has burned out
His tallow truth, and *love,* which above everything must
Cling to word and body, drains, *Wisdom* remains full,
Whole, unrhymable.

Intone them then: *Breadth Circle Desert*
Monarch Month Wisdom not for whatever spell
They generate but for their mere
Inexorable syntax. The eye's movement outward
Claims its huge dominions not by kinship, nor bond
Of common ending.

KRANICH AND BACH
(A brand of piano no longer made)

Under her golden willow a golden crane
Hangs over golden water, stencilled on the
Heavy lamplit brown of the solemn upright:

Silence standing in a pool of reflection?
Or, if the brook's waters rumble darkly on,
Silence reflecting by a flow of music?

No golden harp with golden wires depends from
The vaulted branch on the shiny varnished ground,
Mirroring the ebony and ivory,

And the glint of golden from a wedding-band,
And the earnest hands of my poor father, who
With forgotten fingers played as best he could,

Muttering, or even roaring out the texts:
Erl-King strokes the boy; trout die in their now-dulled
Stream; the wan Double carries on in moonlight;

Impatience stutters on the keys; water turns
Through its rippling figures, and always the old
Man, bare amid a few tattered chords, still stands

Grinding out his music, *dyum de dum dum dum:*
"Both his feet are bare upon the frozen ground,
In his empty saucer no coin makes a sound."

Lyre-man, I would not know for years that you
Stand at the end of a journey of winter
To be followed only into its silence

As I will follow my father into his.
Dark under the closed lid, Kranich and Bach wait,
Silence standing up one-leggedly in song.

THE MUSE IN THE MONKEY TOWER (Via dei Portoghesi)

for James Wright

American girl, within
Your room up in the tower
Above darkening houses
That squat along darkened streets,
Come to your window or his,
Because it eyes his wider
One which frames it in sunset—

Peer like a kind of day out
Of one region into all
Others, lighting up even
The farrowing street at noon
With what comes out of the dark.
Now while all the visible
Angels rest their stone trumpets

In the hot light, Olive, for
Instance, recollects her brood
Of cloudy doves, passengers
For ages beyond our own:
Ripe-eyed, she keeps all the rest,
But what will come will never
Come of the peaceable hours;

Thus Myrtle, perhaps, our old
Dear substrate, mincing to what
One might dare call her casement,
Would beam admittance to her
Shady bed and a hot fuck
Under the *tramontana:*
What was to come would not cool;

And even Laura, cooler
Than the darkest greens of her
Northwest, waiting for evening
As long as if for ever,
Aureate hair catching a
Brightness from beyond her own,
Leaping from the wider day:

No, that lady will not be
Whistled for, and the comic
Lauro from downstairs, poking
Out of his hole in the wall
Shouting for Massimo, comes
Justly rebuking the wrong
Call directed far too high.

You there who are left, Judith
Or Joan or whoever dwells
In the magic tower now,
Gaze across with eyes of sky
Into the shadowed room where
He waits for what will come and
Seize him as if with your light.

From Town and Country Matters

THE LOSS OF SMYRNA

Sick and weak I lay, as the dreadful winter
Drank my life's last wine, and the dreams of prouder
Days and loud, sweet nights seemed to snap and splinter
Into a powder.

Sick and weak; till then I remembered SMYRNA,
Port of Venus! city of figs and quinces!
Where the poor, tired wanderer yet can earn a
Pleasure of princes.

So I hied me off on an evil steamer,
Crewed by cast-off Lascars, and captained madly.
Mascot mastiffs fought for a human femur;
Cabins smelt badly;

Passengers drugged down far below all sinning
Only made me hungrier for the seaside
Deeply dreamed, whose domes and delights, beginning
Down by the quayside,

Reach away back up into hidden altars
Where the sacrifices to final pleasure
By the one, dark ardor that never falters
Last beyond measure.

Borne thus bravely over despairing's ocean
By the wild, bright dream of those domes, and reaching
Port at last, I joyed at the end of motion,
Firmness of beaching.

But no domes saw I! It was like Biloxi,
Mississippi! I was dismayed and nearly
Screamed 'Oi Weh! Izmir!' But a passing doxy
(She'd gone to Brearley

Thence to Radcliffe), speaking in pear-shaped diphthongs
Said, 'Why this *is* Smyrna, dearie!' and quoting
Other poems by Auden, unlaced her hip-thongs
Slowly emoting.

Moonlit twin domes gleamed then! And oriental
Towers rose; courts; gardens that seem to burn a
Flame within my memory still! No mental
Yearning, but SMYRNA!

Then she led me back to an ancient quarter
Where the town's joys lay, to a house where seven
Sisters who looked each like the others' daughter
Guarded a heaven.

Seven? Nay, more nearly a hundred ladies
Filled that Empyrean with their equipment,
Bubbling, tossed, twitched, jouncing; and half of Hades,
Ready for shipment,

Waited down boats' holds or in lazaretted
Cellars near Seine, Thames, or the Rhine's conflation
Hard by Basel—maidens awaiting fêted
Pleasure's purgation.

There the rainbow pales in ashamed abasement
Under such wide, variegated spectra!
Antique illustrations in every casement:
Reddened Electra

There goes down on a yet-arrested brother,
Bound and lashed; and Circe outdoes herself there:
Half her own sex, turned into half another,
Over a shelf there.

Visions! dreams! joys! promises of eternal
Freedoms! bondages far beyond describing
Catalogued on welcoming flasks of Smyrnal
Things for imbibing.

There the warm will stints not, and there the flesh is
Even more than eager for overreaching,
Where a white form, crossed with the crimson meshes
Shows the rod's teaching.

There, too, Spring and Fall are maintained together
Both at once, as in every perfect Bower:
Nine-year-olds and their grandpas play touch-feather
Hour by hour.

Frontal voyagings! and severe excursions
Into backward countries, where dark, unmasking
Secrets yield themselves! even furred diversions!
—All for the asking.

Vast, complex arrangements for feet: a fire,
Heating steel shoes (there are so many martyrs!)
And, to draw those torturing buskins higher,
Horrible garters!

Even you, dear friend, looking down to greet me
From a balcony over someone's shoulder
(She, the meanwhile, wriggling) appeared to meet me
Looking much bolder

Than you have ever been. As I moved, saluting,
Suddenly Night fell—not a night of blisses
Filled with Smyrning raptures—but reedy fluting,
Turning to hisses,

Surged behind my temples and—blink and swallow—
There I lay. Cold winter had just uncrowned me.
SMYRNA? Gone! gone in a vision's hollow
            Smashing around me.

Where again shall pain be redeemed in blessings?
Where else may we see such a fierce, a stern, a
Hard and iron touch make such sweet caressings?
            Where, but in SMYRNA!

When again in dream or in sickly vision
Shall I, then, with thirteen young ladies turn a
Banquet into such a complex elision?
            Never in SMYRNA!

NEW YORK

Quid Romae faciam . . . —JUVENAL, SAT. III

*'Sing of New York, the—*what?' *exclaimed the Muse,*
'My dear, you're kidding!' and turned to refuse
My true, caressing hand between her thighs
(An Argo sailing toward his golden prize).
She wiggled some, and pouted ever so,
And then those thighs swung shut against the foe.
Her legs lay parallel along the sheet
Like lines in couplets that can never meet,
Being but intersected by their rhyme
As if to say: 'No poem for you this time,
No founts, no depths of form from me tonight,
No sea-shapes and no rhythms wrung from light.
Go back to all that cultivated patter
Of rhymed iambics, and to subject matter.
"New York"—that's folly that I can't endure.
No poem: you'll have to give them literature.
And I've got better things to do.' She rose,
Dressed, cursed a zipper that refused to close,
Checked the hem of her interstellar dress
And ran off, to those better things, I guess.

Farewell! My dear old friend is leaving town
At last; and if I say this with a frown
Not of expected loss, but of chagrin
(He's running out, just as I'm moving in),
It's not because I don't admire the way
His urban night awakes to purer day:
Despite the bleakness of most rural sights,
Choose Adirondack over Brooklyn Heights,
Better in solitude than fear to dwell,
To yawn in heaven, than explode in hell:

Bombed houses falling on your head, crossed wires,
Rich young folks piously igniting fires,
Poisonous traffic, air awash with crud,
And august poets bawling out for blood.

His groaning U-Haul halted at the spot—
In view of Hell-Gate's vaulted arch—where not
One car a minute really can survive
From ninety-sixth street to the east side drive,
My old friend Rus got out, sat on the hood
Of his Detroit Disgusting; near him stood,
Sooty and pale, bland-visaged as a dumb thing,
A ghastly hospital—or school—or something;
A clogged, unmoving stream of traffic hid
The sluggish, filthy river as it slid
Between the welfare islands on both banks;
Smokestacks gazed down at air-enhancing tanks.
Surveying his belongings crammed within
His orange trailer—an old mandolin;
Ten yards of tweeds he'd once brought home from Nassau;
His crated Greek pot; and his Ibram Lassaw
(And what, crammed in between his carpet slippers,
One would guess was a pair of coupon-clippers)
Part of his wardrobe; lamps; an indiscreet
Case of real '49 Chateau Lafite
He'd never broken out for me; the pearls
Of a small shell collection; his ex-girl's
Pre-amplifier and my *Lohengrin*
Leered through lacunae in the tarpaulin.

He sighed and shrugged: 'There's no more room for me.
I'm broke, and, like the air, whatever's free
Is probably poisonous: I'm off to green
Lawns wider than a color TV screen.
I've had it all; let those remain who need
The grinding crowds and the great mills of greed:

The thieving steel of the Triborough Bridge
Authority spans Pelham and Bay Ridge,
Whose Moses may have slain an overseer
Once long ago—but see his late career,
Cornering the straw market, and his boast,
Outliving Pharaohs, a rich palace ghost.
Let grasping landlords stay to plead and whimper,
And builders, whose new walls each day grow limper.
Let him who must, remain: the poorest wretch,
Chained by his indigence to a bleak stretch
Of asphalt turf; the richest, too, must stay,
Chained just to his ability to pay.

'What's in New York for me? A clever liar
I'm not, whether for purchase or for hire.
The quarrelsome and unconvivial cup
Of parties bores me, and I am fed up
With agitprop. I'm unemployable
At praising cheesey books because they're *full*
Of where it's at right now! The theatre's shit:
Broadway twaddle is only aimed to twit
The pudding sensibilities of dumb
Women, unliberated yet, who come
From out of town (or in: it doesn't make
The slightest bit of difference) and take
The seats, and as demeaning audience, the cake.
—Or go off-off-off Broadway, way down east:
You'll find it isn't better in the least.
There, "theatre must engage its viewers" and
Break down the evil boundaries that stand
Between the shower and the being shown;
Playgoers now cannot be left alone,
And so unlovely boys and solemn drabs
Mix with the audience, and give them crabs,
While "interpenetration" is so literal
It must involve the phallic and the clitoral.

Critics? They don't need me. Somewhere they'll find
Some venomous tongue, led by a minor mind
To drop, while snarling like an animal,
Yugo-Hungarian poison on it all.

'It's all too much. The old Metropolis
Was never planned to be the Bower of Bliss.
But crowding, cosmopolitan manure,
Meant that some civilization was secure:
Enough intelligent people, living in
Enough proximity, so that the din
Of louder-than-ordinary life around
Confused and comforted one with the sound.
The idiot driver's leaned-on, angry horn,
Failing to goad the beast on which he's borne,
The smashing of non-operative telephone,
Squealing of brakes, totalitarian drone
Of sirens rushing to elicit ire
With rude contempt, or to put out a fire—
Noises of busyness make their retreats
As yowling chaos reassumes the streets.'

He ceased as, through the halted traffic's mass,
A nodding youth of fourteen dragged his ass
Past a stalled ambulance, then, beyond pain,
Vanished near where a gutter may have lain.
'Diacetyl morphine, sad heroine!'
My friend continued, 'you whose only sin
Was to submit to Harrison's foul sway!
Golden and sanguine laws which tempt and slay
Forbidding, make desired and most dear
In price, what otherwise we might not fear.
Pork-barrel legislation for the mob
Keeps many a bribed narc in his nasty job.
Her sad and not unwitting victims dot
The streets, while moralists inspect their lot,

Weep, and conclude that in this happy isle
All prospects please, and only junk is vile.

'Ill fares the land that merits little praise,
Where men accumulate, and wealth decays;
Where Mulciber & Sons, Incorporated,
Builders of pre-fab ruins, unabated
Spawn their impermanent boxes everywhere,
Pasting their cheapness on the dusty air.
Imperial Rome was splendid, if confused,
But useful buildings really could be used.
Now bricklayers, plying their ancient art,
Muck up their mortar from the very start,
Take coffee breaks all day, and with a chuckle
Watch as the walls they build begin to buckle.'
He paused to watch a tired patrolman shove
One of the public he was servant of,
Who bellowed back at his blue-coated brother;
Each tried for greater rudeness than the other.
Back to his car-hood and his theme Rus leapt:
'Service, each month more grudging and inept,
Has sovietized: the languages I speak
Are only English, German, French, some Greek,
Italian, Yiddish and a bit of Gullah—
I never needed them to get a cruller
And coffee, or to give a street address:
I'm not so good at Spanish, I confess,
And so in cabs I circle through the dark
When all I wished was to traverse the park.
I'm threatened when the tip's not twice the fare.
But then, I wasn't going anywhere,
Really, just to the movies, to await
For forty minutes, freezing at the gate,
Three hours'—not dollars'—worth of naked snatch,
Amplified panting and a pilfered batch
Of glossy travel shots, with twanging sounds,

Like pharmaceuticals, making the rounds
Among an audience whose tepid praise
Is touched by memories of milder days
When Wittgenstein, and I, flicked out each night
At something mindless, beautiful and bright.'

Well, how about the Mets? They have come far . . .
'—The Mets? The Museum and the Opera?
Then, no, until the angels start to sing
At the departure of Director Bing
When there will vanish, with a mighty roar,
His audience, productions and decor.
Across the park, the other Met is ill:
You can find pots and pictures in it still
I guess, among the crowds who are lured in
Not by the touching, bronze-age safety pin,
The Dirck Bouts, or the Hellenistic head,
Beauties and truths of the unending dead,
But by the price-tag on the latest purchase.
While guards now eye us warily, and search us
For razors, car antennae, pots of grease
With which mobs humanize a masterpiece,
The Mammon of attendance figures stands
Rubbing his failing directorial hands.
Dear Hoving! let him repossess with love
Those parks he was a good commissioner of!

'Richmond and Queens? all that's a world apart
That neither touches, nor yet breaks my heart.
While evil flourishes in Washington
My loud, minority New York's the one
I'm leaving—where disgusting Mitchell breeds
Allies like flies whose hopeless, violent deeds
Augment his power; so I'm off to where
Queens is diluted in a lot of air.
Truth is in hiding, language so decayed

That I can't say I call a spade a spade
Without a chorus of *"You see, you see!*
Languageists are the real enemy!"

'Manhattan's all there is, and that's no good—
There's no equivalent of St. John's Wood.
I don't belong to the quasurban faction:
One passive sufferer in the realm of action,
Sebastian, seems to flourish in St. George,
S.I., where once the smithy's sounding forge
Rang out above the bay—a gurgling tunnel
May soon convert his village to a funnel.
We're had by that great powerful, con Ed:
Bell's ads are lively, but their phones are dead.
Call "Operator" and you can expect
A surly girl, and with a speech defect.
Alf moved here from his house on Beacon Hill
And nightly hears, despite his sleeping-pill,
Through his thin walls on Second Avenue
His neighbors quarrel, and his neighbors screw.
His friend Ralph lives on the West Side, meanwhile,
In a well-built, half-century-old pile:
High ceilings, wide rooms out of rooms unfolding,
Where squads of roaches drill along the molding.
Ted has been mugged and Chloe has been raped;
Charles had his left ear messily reshaped;
Twelve burglaries have left poor Colin vexed—
I shall not wait around to be the next.'

Scarce had he reached the end of his complaint,
The foul air making even sunset faint,
When the loud horn, incessant and unkind,
From a pick Ford Omphalos just behind
Urged him behind his wheel; waving goodnight,
Rus vanished in the fading urban light.

My eyes strained after him, a ruby gleam
Of tail-light sinking in a sanguine stream
Stretching across the bridges, reaching out
For green, receding hills which, in the rout
Of growing dust and sinking darkness, fade
Further into the distance each decade.
I turned back toward the city then, to muse
On his bright future, with those shining views
And costly beauties of which we're in want:
Dilapidated walls in cold Vermont;
Impoverished rustics, down the road a piece,
Whose nephew was caught buggering their niece;
White cotton-batting bread for sale at all
(Both) local supermarkets. O, the ball
The firemen (volunteer) contrive each spring!
(You'll know the season's surely—er—in swing.)
Two cars; four snow tires; fifty sets of keys;
Expiring herds of handymen to please;
Forty-mile drives to fan the dying coals
Of conversation with some other souls
Who still remember what discourse can be
Among the few who don't need every 't'
Crossed in bold-face, nor a shared, dubious joint
Gasped at, in order just to grasp the point.

But let me not sip from an empty cup:
Despite such easy, juvenile bitching-up,
Trees are at best drab objects when they take
The place of people (unless you can make,
Like George the Third in his insanity,
Intelligent conversation with a tree).
Mountains are not to climb, but to remember;
Sunset on bare, wide beaches in September,
The chill of brilliant, dark Sierra nights,
Midocean loomings of the Northern Lights,
The closed, familial huddle of small towns

In winter whites, autumnal reds and browns—
All blossoming fictions, plucked just for the day,
Brought home against the truth of urban gray,
Will flower in the garden of the mind,
Their pale originals quite left behind.
But if one's sentenced to a daily view,
Nature will fail him in a day or two.
I who had undergone a banishment
(Fifteen years long in the wrong cities pent)
Replacing my fled counterpart, can sink
Into New York's congestion, fear and stink,
Untilled concrete beneath a dirty dome:
The difference is that I am moving home.
Throughout this country, one's home town contracts
After one leaves it, and remembered facts
Are paler, teachers shorter, neighborhoods
Narrowed and sunken, the beloved woods
One picnicked in a patch of scrubby alder;
Bright shops get dingy, public grass grows balder.
The older shapes of living shrink, and those
Who move among them still like ghosts, enclose
A seeming want of substance: who returns
Home again in America, but burns
With mixed embarrassment and cindered love
For everything he was the upshot of?
New York gets worse, but so does everything.
It hasn't shrunk a bit. What I could bring
Back to the city after fifteen years
Of exile hasn't melted into tears
That, partly condescending, partly fond,
Watered the ground that I had grown beyond.
I surely came back in a rush of luck:
No horrors happened in the mover's truck;
I moved all but a few things which I stored
To an apartment I can still afford
(I am part owner of the flat I rent me).

Ed Koch, my congressman, can represent me
Because there is about as much good sense
Concentrated in his constituents
As there is anywhere; my children go
To un-selfconscious school at home, and so
They feel at home in school—good luck, it's true.
But whether in China or, indeed, Peru,
In small towns, the well-favored and the wretch,
Haven't much room in which their luck can stretch.

In smaller cities, nothing much can be
Private, and all one finds is secrecy.
A crowd is not a mob, nor makes one die
A death of self inside it, with a sigh.
Only in anonymity and crowds
Can urban wanderers unwind their shrouds,
Unchained by nature in their final quest
Where largest, deepest cities are the best.
Green foliage and a backwoods road or two
Hide Appalachian poverty from view:
In the Metropolis, the hopeless poor
Decently plain, are by no means obscure.
High towers with dingy walkups at their backs
Are found disposed on both sides of the tracks;
And even urban rustics, those who live
Not in the city, but in primitive
Villages scattered in among its blight
Are led out, no great distance, into light.

Now as for homecomings—*mirabile factu!*—
New York's the only city to come back to;
Reaching Manhattan, high over the tossed
Water at Spuyten Duyvil which I crossed
Once in a kayak when I was nineteen;
Turbulent thoughts impressed upon its screen
Of surface, glittering with overlaid

Transparencies of memory, filtering shade
And repetitions animate a view
That I am more than just returning to.

Thus I live here again. My brother Mike
Has moved next door; and in a way, I'm like
Some old agrarian conservative:
The half-mile distance between where I live
And where I did when I was ten, feels never
Once like a shackle I should want to sever
Now, but like an extension of my own,
A tap-root run though asphalt, pipe and stone—
Plenty of continuity for an
Otherwise rootless cosmopolitan.
But memory has its hearsay too: my great-
Grandfather came in 1848,
Fleeing from fuzz and new defenestrations
In Prague, to wander here among the nations,
Bring up his dozen children, make cigars,
And live for me in anecdote, like stars,
Those tiny innuendoes, piercing night,
From which a child infers a plain of light.
My grandfather and I walked in the park
Around the frozen lake, in growing dark;
In 1888, he said, the year
Of the great blizzard, we crossed without fear.
I listened as the bundled skaters skimmed
The gray ice on the safe part that was rimmed
With benches, cut across the reflex of
A starry park lamp on the bridge above.
Who was remembering, and who had merely
Heard of the past? For each it gleamed as clearly.

Now nested memories open up again:
My older daughter, at the age of ten.
Hears of the old Met Opera House from me,

Some half-formed fiction she will never see,
As at the same age, I was quite at home
With a remembrance called the Hippodrome—
Phased, similar emblems of the city's quest,
Moving beyond historic palimpsest,
For instant self-fulfillment. One night late,
Six years ago in August, through the great
Newly revealed vaults in a ruined, weird
Penn Station, winds sang and faint stars appeared
Above columnar bases; broken gloom
Swallowed the crystal-palace waiting room
In gaping Piranesian pits—all seemed
Somehow created for this, and redeemed
By that great wind-swept moment. Then I passed
Out onto the hot pavements, to be gassed
By buses, bumped by derelicts, away
From dreams of change to contact with decay.—
But so much more decay because we've got
Riches to moulder, and so much to rot.

Tim lives downtown, and makes a long commute
(To Queens, to work) as long as is the route
Deep into Westchester; he gets to go
Home to a lovely place on Bank Street, though;
Not the benighted suburb, Middle Ridge
Where affluence is underprivilege.
Jim lives in Athens; there's no need to roam;
Our ruins-and-fig republic here at home
Will mellow us, as things go to the bad,
And lend us patience that we've never had.
Then, as our science fails and our arts rot,
Instead of huddling in some minor spot
On the torn outskirts of a little town
(Where more than here, old buildings are torn down,
And metal siding fronts for honest wood)
We'll see the ending out from where we should:

III

With nothing working, services gone slack,
Mushrooms on the abandoned subway track,
Telephones silent between twelve and two,
Thousands of cats reclaim an empty zoo.

West in Manhattan where the sun has set
The elevator rises calmly yet
In my dark tower, against the tower-dimmed sky,
Whose wide, old windows yield my narrower eye
Images no revision can defeat:
Newspapers blown along the empty street
At three A.M. (somewhere in between 'odd,'
A guru told me long ago, and 'God');
Calm steam rising from manholes in the dark;
Clean asphalt of an avenue; the spark
Of gold in every mica window high
On westward faces of the peaks; the sky
Near dawn, framed in the zig-zag canyon rim
Of cross-streets; bits of distant bridge, the dim
Lustrous ropes of pale lights dipping low;
Rivers unseen beneath, sable and slow.

Gardens? Lead me not home to them: a plain
Of rooftops, gleaming after April rain
In later sunlight, shines with Ceres' gold
Sprung up, not ripped, from earth; gained as of old.
Our losses are of gardens. We create
A dense, sad city for our final state.

•

From The Night Mirror

THE NIGHT MIRROR

What it showed was always the same—
A vertical panel with him in it,
Being a horrible bit of movement
At the edge of knowledge, overhanging
The canyons of nightmare. And when the last
Glimpse was enough—his grandmother,
Say, with a blood-red face, rising
From her Windsor chair in the warm lamplight
To tell him something—he would scramble up,
Waiting to hear himself shrieking, and gain
The ledge of the world, his bed, lit by
The pale rectangle of window, eclipsed
By a dark shape, but a shape that moved
And saw and knew and mistook its reflection
In the tall panel on the closet door
For itself. The silver corona of moonlight
That gloried his glimpsed heard was enough
To send him back into silences (choosing
Fear in those chasms below), to reject
Freedom of wakeful seeing, believing
And feeling, for peace and the bondage of horrors
Welling up only from deep within
That dark planet head, spinning beyond
The rim of the night mirror's range, huge
And cold, on the pillow's dark side.

UNDER CANCER

On the Memorial building's
Terrace the sun has been buzzing
Unbearably, all the while
The white baking happens
To the shadow of the table's
White-painted iron. It darkens,
Meaning that the sun is stronger,
That I am invisibly darkening
Too, the while I whiten.
And only after the stretching
And getting up, still sweating,
My shirt striped like an awning
Drawn on over airlessness;
After the cool shades
(As if of a long arcade
Where footsteps echo gravely)
Have devoured the light;
Only after the cold of
Plunge and shower, the pale
Scent of deodorant stick
Smelling like gin and limes,
And another stripy shirt
Can come, homing in at last,
The buzzing of having been burnt.
Only then, intimations
Of tossing, hot in the dark
Night, where all the long while
Silently, along edges,
There is flaking away.

In this short while of light
My shadow darkens without
Lengthening ever, ever.

AD MUSAM

O my Dear,
I have been getting it all
Wrong about us for so
Many a year;

I have presented you
With all that I thought I had
To give: small boxes; my water
Colors of blue

Ocean; some truer
Photographs of pitch darkness
I let expose through the night;
Blue beads, and bluer

Papery flowers
I bought in a bad boutique
On a somewhat dangerous street,
Long after hours;

Meals I have made
You—soups that brooded for weeks,
Blossom pies; curried rememberings and
Mauve lemonade;

Pawn tickets (two),
One for a bright, green object
Whose shape I forget, and one for a
Picture of you;

My winnings at cards
That summer I only won
One game; my nautilus shell;
Several yards

Of peacock and gold
Brocade; my many-stringed
Archlute; half of my ice-cream,
Sweet and still cold, . . .

I gave. I recall.
Drop by corrosive drop,
Through these holes in my memory
Ah, how they fall

Gifts that seemed the measure
Of giving: I wished to withhold
Nothing, but thought to spare you the
Trash.—Or the Treasure

Perhaps? As I cross
The graying December park in
A wind that shrieks and sunders,
Doubled with loss

And straightforward motion,
I approach the evening of Autumn
And stumble on something sunk in the
Sheep-Meadow's ocean,

Something like mud,
That shone once, now turned to what
Reads, by this vast, dim lamp as the
Color of blood.

Love, love, take
This lost blob I'd keep not
For my own, or for other alms, or for
Keeping's sake,

But had only hid
For unknowing of worth, for want
Of age, for mistaking yours.
Now I am rid

Of present giving:
This is our season, Bright Sister.
We are both of an age; I'll not spend it
Loving, but living

Your life, and you, mine.
Now! Snowflakes! as if inside
The cold of the whole dark globe, the
Fire of nine

Fictions were flinging
Light; as if frozen sparks
Leap downward as they surround me,
Dancing and singing.

AT THE NEW YEAR

Every single instant begins another new year;
Sunlight flashing on water, or plunging into a clearing
In quiet woods announces; the hovering gull proclaims
Even in wide midsummer a point of turning: and fading
Late winter daylight close behind the huddled backs
Of houses close to the edge of town flares up and shatters
As well as any screeching ram's horn can, wheel
Unbroken, uncomprehended continuity,
Making a starting point of a moment along the way,
Spinning the year about one day's pivot of change.
But if there is to be a high moment of turning
When a great, autumnal page, say, takes up its curved
Flight in memory's spaces, and with a final sigh,
As of every door in the world shutting at once, subsides
Into the bed of its fellows; if there is to be
A time of tallying, recounting and rereading
Illuminated annals, crowded with black and white
And here and there a capital flaring with silver and bright
Blue, then let it come at a time like this, not at winter's
Night, when a few dead leaves crusted with frost lie shivering
On our doorsteps to be counted, or when our moments of coldness
Rise up to chill us again. But let us say at a golden
Moment just on the edge of harvesting, "Yes. Now."
Times of counting are times of remembering; here amidst showers
Of shiny fruits, both the sweet and the bitter-tasting results,
The honey of promises gleams on apples that turn to mud
In our innermost of mouths, we can sit facing westward
Toward imminent rich tents, telling and remembering.

THE BIRD

from the Yiddish of Moishe Leib Halpern

Well, this bird comes, and under his wing is a crutch,
And he asks why I keep my door on the latch;
So I tell him that right outside the gate
Many robbers watch and wait
To get at the hidden bit of cheese,
Under my ass, behind my knees.

Then through the keyhole and the crack in the jamb
The bird bawls out he's my brother Sam,
And tells me I'll never begin to believe
How sorely he was made to grieve
On shipboard, where he had to ride
Out on deck, he says, from the other side.

So I get a whiff of what's in the air,
And leave the bird just standing there.
Meanwhile—because one never knows,
I mean—I'm keeping on my toes,
Further pushing my bit of cheese
Under my ass and toward my knees.

The bird bends his wing to shade his eyes
—Just like my brother Sam—and cries,
Through the keyhole, that *his* luck should shine
Maybe so blindingly as mine,
Because, he says, he's seen my bit
Of cheese, and he'll crack my skull for it.

It's not so nice here anymore.
So I wiggle slowly towards the door,
Holding my chair and that bit of cheese
Under my ass, behind my knees,
Quietly. But then as if I care,

I ask him whether it's cold out there.

They are frozen totally,
Both his poor ears, he answers me,
Declaring with a frightful moan
That, while he lay asleep alone
He ate up his leg—the one he's lost.
If I let him in, I can hear the rest.

When I hear the words "ate up", you can bet
That I'm terrified; I almost forget
To guard my bit of hidden cheese
Under my ass there, behind my knees.
But I reach below and, yes, it's still here,
So I haven't the slightest thing to fear.

Then I move that we should try a bout
Of waiting, to see which first gives out,
His patience, there, behind the door,
Or mine, in my own house. And more
And more I feel it's funny, what
A lot of patience I have got.

And that's the way it's stayed, although
That was some seven years ago.
I still call out "Hi, there!" through the door.
He screams back " 'Lo there" as before.
"Let me out" I plead, "don't be a louse"
And he answers, "Let me in the house".

But I know what he wants. So I bide
My time and let him wait outside.
He enquires about the bit of cheese
Under my ass, behind my knees;
Scared, I reach down, but, yes, it's still here.
I haven't the slightest thing to fear.

THE WILL

from the Yiddish of Moishe Leib Halpern

Now this is how I did myself in:
No sooner did the sun begin
To shine, when I was up and away,
Gathering goat-shit for my tune
—The one I wrote just yesterday
About the moonlight and the moon—
And then I put with these also
Some poems from my portfolio
In re the bible's sanctity
(Just thinking of them sickens me)
And these I wrapped up in my rag
Of an old coat, packed up like a bag,
After which, I took the whole shebang
Put up a nail, and let it hang
Outside my window, on a tray.
Adults and children passed my way
And asked what that mess up there could be,
So I answered them, on bended knee:
These are all my years; I think
They went all rotten with infection
By wisdom, and its ancient stink,
From my precious book collection.
But when my son, the little boy,
(In my sea of sorrow and cup of joy
He's just turned four) strained his eyes to see
Those summits of sublimity,
Well—I put him on my knee
And spake thus: Harken thou to me,
My son and heir, I swear that, just
As none disturb the dead in their rest,
So, when you have finally grown,
I'll leave you thoroughly alone.
Want to be a loan-shark, a bagel-lifter?

Be one, my child.
Want to murder, set fires, or be a grifter?
Be one, my child.
Want to change off girls with the speed that those
Same girls keep changing their own clothes?
Change away, my child.
But one thing, child, I have to say:
If once ambition leads you to try
To make some kind of big display
Of yourself with what's hanging up there in the sky;
If you dare (but may that time not come soon!)
To write about moonlight and the moon,
Or some poem of the bible, poisoning the world,
Then, my dear,
If I'm worth something then by way of any
Money, so much as a single penny,
I'll make my will, leaving everything
To my *Landsman,* the future Polish King.
Though we've both stopped calling each other "thou",
I'll chop up, like a miser shredding
Cake for beggars at a wedding,
All the ties that yet bind us now.
Poppa-chopper Son-schmon
And so help me God in Heaven
This
Will
Be
Done.

LETTER TO JORGE LUIS BORGES: APROPOS OF THE GOLEM

I've never been to Prague, and the last time
That I was there its stones sang in the rain;
The river dreamed them and that dream lay plain
Upon its surface, shallow and sublime.

The residues of years of dream remained
Solidified in structures on each bank;
Other dreams than of Prague and Raining sank
Under dark water as their memory waned.

And far beneath the surface of reflection
Lay a deep dream that was not Prague, but of it,
Of silent light from the gray sky above it,
The river running in some dreamed direction.

O Borges, I remember this too clearly—
Staring at paper now, having translated
Your poem of Prague, my flood of ink abated—
To have recalled it from my last trip, merely.

Three mythical cronies my great-grandfather
Was known to speak of nurture dark designs
Against my childhood: from between the lines
Of what was told me of them, I infer

How Haschele Bizensis, Chaim Pip,
The Bab Menucha and his friends, conspire
Over old pipes; sparks in a beard catch fire,
The smoke grows heavier with each slow sip . . .

I scream and wake from sleep into a room
I only remember now in dreams; my mother

Calms me with tales of Prague back in another
Time. All I remember is a tomb

Near what was called the Old-New Synagogue;
Under a baroque stone whose urn and column
Emerge in the first dawn lies, dead and solemn,
My ancestor, the Rabbi Loew of Prague.

He made The Golem (which means "embryo,"
"Potential person," much more than "machine")
And quickened him with a Name that has been
Hidden behind all names that one could know.

We have our family secrets: how the creature
Tried for the Rabbi's daughter, upped her dress
Till nacreous and bushy nakedness
Shone in the moonlight; groped; but failed to reach her—

How once, when heat throbbed in the August skies
And children were playing hide-and-seek, the Golem
Trailed the one who was It, and nearly stole him
Before the shadows rang with all their cries.

But was he circumcised? What glimmerings rose
In his thick face at evening? Were they sham?
Did he and nine men make a quorum? I am
Not, alas, at liberty to disclose.

(But how he saved the Jews of Prague is told
In a late story—from a Polish source?—
Not to be taken seriously, of course,
No more than one about the Emperor's gold.)

These tales jostle each other in their corner
At the eye's edge, skirting the light of day
(The Bab Menucha lurks not far away,

As if around a grave, like a paid mourner).

Too dumb to live, he could not touch, but muddy:
Lest the virgin Sabbath be desecrated,
The rabbi spoke. It was deanimated;
Half-baked ceramic moldered in his study . . .

Save for the Fire of process, elements
Mix sadly: Mud is born of Water and Earth;
Air knows Water—a bubble comes to birth;
Earth and Air—nothing that makes any sense.

But bubble, mud and that incoherent third,
When animated by the Meta-Name
That is no mere breath of air itself, became
The myth whose footsteps we just overheard

Together, shuffling down a hallway, Borges,
Toward its own decreation, dull and lonely,
Lost in the meager world of one and only
One Golem, but so many Johns and Jorges.

GRANNY SMITH

Deep, fallen azure she flashes,
Of the grass sky beneath our feet
Untoppled yet—the greeny one,
Waiting among the usual
Fruits of our life. And why I had
Not thought to find her here among
Apples of the earth and sun, the
Bright Americans fallen or
Plucked, was: why, freshening ever
On her fable of tree, she fell
To harvest merely; why she turned
Skull-color as the dark witch dipped
Her into something bubbling; why
She dropped, green levin, to her grave
From Newton's skyward tree; why pierced
Marbles of eyes roll up in sleep,
Thin-lidded, toward the patient dark.

EVENING WOLVES

Generality of white light at Creation
Blindly contracted into mere orbs of yellow
Sun and cool of moon and of icier
Starlight. But where does it hang, the spore

Left of this narrowed blue? Midwinter wolves running
Under such final light flash signals from something
Blue like the false ball of an eye which is
That of no wolf, but is his who wields

Blues of the cold alone; of hurrying lateness,
Shortness of north and its furthest dark hours;
Blue not of sky ice, but of whiteness of
Grayness of wolf. And of other wolves

As in a rush of judgment, sudden from shadows,
Stopped, like the icy axe of a frozen comber
Midcrested, edging some condemned, empty
Shore. These are shadows of blue of wolves

Under the pine-broken verge the line of sky makes
With the wide, distant ice that our gaze had strained for:
Blue not of high eyes, but of blindness of
Failure. Of wolf. An indented line

Bares the blue light unfallen, general, coldly
Creating only itself. Pelted in thunder,
Hard-eared, like wandering stars they skim these
Dimmed, clouded fields, this blackness of blue.

DAMOETAS

In memory of Andrew Chiappe,
teacher of Shakespeare, dead in France
May, 1967.

I

The birth of a middle year
Lies not in the buried tube of pinched
First months, but later in the clear
Leap into green being. Spring
Has delivered a new age now, and death
Shall flash into flower on every hedge,
For it is a gray
May: we have reached the edge
Of one more stream to be crossed
One way only into these broad,
Lean fields of grief, all speech lost
In buzzing, unmown silences,
Thick with the ticking of countless watches.
And in our middle, listening time
We hear each death
As the hard echo of our breath
And read the shapes of sorrow in
The shadows of the smothering, high
Cumulus that scud across
The bottom of an unwatched sky,
Yielding no sobs of rain.
Our teachers have started leaving.
Our fields are darkening, and late
Flies wind an autumnal horn
As we pause at the unlatched gate;
But it is grief alone
That leads us to loitering among the fictions:
Distractions of fields by water,

Thoughts of memorial stone,
Wide courts, triumphant swans, and pale reflections.

2

This was too heavy a spring, the April
Vacant, the conditional May
Shattered with cold, and now old
Damoetas dead: and suddenly thereby
Our dying has commenced, and dry
Languages of mourning hold
Fast in their unfilled beds,
Stony and motionless, used up. And
Praise? It frays in our sharpened,
Shiny, ironic machines. And Plaint?
It will water nothing that has really dried.
And Explaining who a teacher was
Is wearyingly like
Expounding unopened volumes of self
Aloud to a dusty, silent hall
Dim with disbelief, in a late
Afternoon at the end of fall.

Damoetas dead: back from treading
Some of his own youthful fields, I see
Some white sheet bleaching on the edge
Of hay piled up and distant trees; I see
As through the green spikes and hidden white
Of the distant-flowered sedge,
Down an oracular canal,
The noblest and the brassiest
Impresa of gawkiness redeemed,
And beauty whose terminal
Is eloquence, floats on the gleaming
Water. Swans, though, do not sing at last;
Posthumous, unlocked pages shred

In eager fingers; and the dead,
Still in their silent past,
Gowned in remembrances, the dons undone
Stroll on their long lawns across
The narrow river from us.

Now noon. And evening soon; but stand
Here, for a space, with death ascendant
On the green bank, a low bridge on each hand,
With dropped eyes, O annual, grand
Tourist: Watch all the arch, old emblems fall
Into a processional
Sequence of watery reflections
Under an intermittent sun,
And then go westward home,
Lest the learned gestures,
Laughing and dancing on a shaded lawn,
Draw you back with a caress
Toward shallow deeps
And suddenly empty pastures
Along that dreaming stream, which keeps
Only the shadows that will soon be gone.

3

Echoes of all elegies
Sounded what I had to say
As my breath was sucked away
When the winds rose on the seas.

I remembered breathlessness
In a warm and windless room,
Windowing November gloom,
Bright with his attentiveness.

White hands darted in the air;
Meanings, seized like fireflies
Flashing in our summer skies,
Fell on green minds everywhere.

Ancient cadences return:
Meadows of the gray concrete
Soft beneath our rapid feet
Echo as within an urn;

Lowing trolley-cars once more
Clatter homeward, while nearby
Fiery sirens tear the sky
From the city's threshing-floor.

Evening constellations; pied
Neon clouds among their gold;
Flocks of hope head for a fold
High in sweet, bleak Morningside.

Sunsets drop behind the park
Where the wide, wide river runs;
Wondering boys, whose eyes like suns,
Dazzle as they face the dark—

Mustapha and Portugal
Bobby and Farouk, struck by
That wide, unattending eye,
Aimed beyond the visual,

Hoping to discern a brief
Round significance some night,
Catch it up, and pluck a bright
Global dewdrop from a leaf.

Brightness rises from the burned:
Phoenix and the firefly
Flame eternally, and die
Only while the page is turned.

4

Now summer slips away
Between green banks: water,
Swans and distances under a curving dark
Of stone bridge lingering around a bend,
As high, bright noon goes gray and dull
And cancelled shadows
Of our movement over meadows
Only appear lingering for a while
Among other reflections
Before the late and future rain.

But high in summer, even,
Beyond this old, narrow park,
Full in the shining day,
What could Shadow have to say
To Sunlight, about the dark
Massiveness of substance
Intervening, as an opaque
Parent come between the shade
And its radiant creator?
Shadows keep their silences
In life as in death later:
As in water, lain on meadow.

Past lawn, on meadow, we have been
Walking by water, in the chill
Of afternoon, remembering stone,
Then startled by pale orchid stars
Thrust upward through a thickening green

Of autumn grass: the meadow saffron,
Ghost of the crocus, haunting fields
Of dalliance that will yet
In the green winter, blear and wet,
Remain like ripe, ungathered grain.

Meanwhile across the broadest water
A land away westward, home, the pale
Golden grass and the dun
Bones of the grass lie dismembered,
Unquickened in the dumbly wintering sun.

ADAM'S TASK

And Adam gave names to all cattle, and
to the fowl of the air, and to every
beast of the field . . . Gen. 2:20

Thou, paw-paw-paw; thou, glurd; thou, spotted
  Glurd; thou, whitestap, lurching through
The high-grown brush; thou, pliant-footed,
  Implex; thou, awagabu.

Every burrower, each flier
  Came for the name he had to give:
Gay, first work, ever to be prior,
  Not yet sunk to primitive.

Thou, verdle; thou, McFleery's pomma;
  Thou; thou; thou—three types of grawl;
Thou, flisket; thou, kabasch; thou, comma-
  Eared mashawk; thou, all; thou, all.

Were, in a fire of becoming,
  Laboring to be burned away,
Then work, half-measuring, half-humming,
  Would be as serious as play.

Thou, pambler; thou, rivarn; thou, greater
  Wherret, and thou, lesser one;
Thou, sproal; thou, zant; thou, lily-eater.
  Naming's over. Day is done.

From Types of Shape

O with what key
shall I unlock this
heart Tight in a coffer
of chest something awaits a
jab a click a sharp turn yes an
opening Out with it then Let it
pour into forms it molds itself
Much like an escape of dreaming
prisoners taking shape out in a
relenting air in bright volumes
unimaginable even amid anterior
blacknesses let mine run out in
the sunny roads Let them be
released by modulations
of point by bend of
line too tiny for
planning out back
in hopeful dark
times or places
How to hold on
to a part flat
or wide enough
to grasp was
not too hard
formerly and
patterned
edges cut
themselves
What midget
forms shall
fall in
line or
row beyond
this wall
of self A
key can
open a car
Why not me
O let me
get in

SKELETON KEY

Opening and starting key for a 1954 Dodge junked last year.

I have given up caring whether youre genuine or not
now that I know what you have been through Slowly
shortening moments of course but the harsh snap
of the speeded-up instant and the rape of the
smooth black surface like a cracked shellac
record are authentic enough While you say
I TOO WAS EARTH ONCE STILL I YIELDED UP
FORMS POSSIBLE IN ME TO TURN MERE CUP
your fault your cracked base cannot
be seen from where I look and try
to read your heart And what you
say is true enough for mortals or
for earthen gods What bears
the weight of this so
pretentious
crown Is it
mere mire
column of
common or
even rare
clay that
carries a
proud cup
so dry so
empty now
Lo what the
potter twists
on his flat
turning wheel
is his idea and
a cup or an image
a poem or body that
turns beneath my hand O
beauty is no less true than you

A POSSIBLE FAKE

Black, undecorated bucchero cup, cracked and mended,
Etruscan, bought in Rome 1963 with no questions asked.

On or
off Either darkness
unlocked again or feigned
daylight perhaps graded only by
stepped intensities fifty watts apart
In any event no continuities like those
of flickering no nor even of fading Flick
Click and there it is suddenly Oh yes I see
Indeed A mind hung brilliantly upon filaments
stung by some untongued brightness opening up
also encloses and the dark unbounded room lit
by bare bulbs collapses into an unhurting box
occupied by furniture now avoidable The dot
of closure menaces the attention which in
the flutter of eyelids can only tremble
like a nervous child lying awake lest
he be aware of the moment a closing
shutter of sleep claps to But a
snapped-off dream disperses
into darkness like gold
becoming mere motes
becoming light If
the eye lies open
to such dust as
sunlight brings
it will never
burn But that
creation make
a visible big
difference in
the way minds
look a shaper
will burn
outwardly
first and
thus once
there was
light

IDEA

Old Mazda lamp, 50-100-150 W.

CRISE DE COEUR

Help me
O help me for only
a brief while ago I hung red
and yet erect in the world of wide
white reticent backgrounds against which
I registered Correctly placed as if pointing
out a direction downwards towards which all must
fall I stood firm I beat out the cut time which we
always hope we have to count on More surely than as an
emblem cut into a thick-skinned tree transfixed by a dart
perhaps I shone and signified Being all crimson and heraldic
as I was and near-kin to the promiscuous scarlet pips of cards
I was unyielding and if conventional than surely constant But as
I stood in my round-shouldered pride you struck Some fell impulse
seized me as if for a moment the surface I clung to had gone blank
like that As if a glimpse of folded arm or breast or thigh curved
under itself plunging deep into its own shadow had unhung me quite
Or as if some loss as of dry leaves blown across marble corridors
was felt for an instant even while unseen I fell tripping over a
minute lapse in lifes surface I fell heavily ah indeed flipped
over and now I lie bleeding on my sheet a sick valentine who
short of breath can barely sigh BE MINE before I fail for
even the short while that will be forever Lying here I
have blackened some and paled Yet recognizable for
what I am and unable to leap I rest uneasy Fever
warms me up towards evening after failure of
nerve has made a noon too bright to bear
bringing in place of sleep a sense
of something wrong something
half-unbroken Like
a heart

A
bit
of an
image a
hint only
a momentary
finial like a
barely-glimpsed
porpoise possibly
thrusting a dark shining horn through the distant water These
should plunge one into the deeps of significance where tall
forms stand for their maker while tides throb vast beyond
dreaming even overhead Craving the rich dark icons ever
denied us one day I drew upon the flat wet sand above
the menace of foamy conquerings this hexagram which
with the broad menorahs feathered wings was all
the symbol we were permitted But far from the
water of summer the sea I would gaze at the
woven equilaterals on the synagogue wall at
the New Year their members joined arms locked
in legs all fondly wrought and standing for and
on the wall unshielding be it in blue or yellow O a
flat emblem almost a blank But as a coupling of these
identicals used so as to seem at war how much a sign of
love Even here though the image dives down into the wider
part to vanish into meaning Here too in my crude making the
end the remembered part before darkness marks a point of love
Let there be only
this final sign
this triangle
of the dark
about thy
opening
loves
own
V

GRAVEN IMAGE

The shield of David, of no great antiquity
as a liturgical symbol.

Dusk
Above the
water hang the
loud
flies
Here
O so
gray
then
What A pale signal will appear
When Soon before its shadow fades
Where Here in this pool of opened eye
In us No Upon us As at the very edges
of where we take shape in the dark air
this object bares its image awakening
ripples of recognition that will
brush darkness up into light
even after this bird this hour both drift by atop the perfect sad instant now
already passing out of sight
toward yet-untroubled reflection
this image bears its object darkening
into memorial shades Scattered bits of
light No of water Or something across
water Breaking up No Being regathered
soon Yet by then a swan will have
gone Yes out of mind into what
vast
pale
hush
of a
place
past
sudden dark as
if a swan
sang

SWAN AND SHADOW

The last shape.

From Visions from the Ramble

WAITING

The air grew hushed at the Flushing Meadows Fair grounds; purple
Residues of sunset vanished in the west; we crowded about
The largest water to watch the illuminations. Pale
Feathers of fountain thrust upwards; from beyond the Lagoon of Nations
Something roared and "Boys and Girls Together" beeped out
From orange carts behind the watchers on the water.
They waited to see what would happen to the fountains. Alf and Ralph
Got lost in the crowd and had to be searched for. Suddenly

A hissing and unseen serpent arose behind the blocks of
Red brick buildings on Eliot Square, hushed by the fleece
Of evening heat, its high trajectory lifting it
Above the Common into the black and boundless sky.
In the gleam of neon epistemologists, talking about
Nextness, moved out off the sidewalk, and craned their necks, just as

Sparklers crackled coolly in the moist dark garden.
Children stood in a ring with bits of punk, peering
Over the glint of magnesium for glimpses of each other's faces;
But just in time to frighten the four-year-old, from beyond

The gray stadium was hushed as the stone benches grew
Colder and the unpromising western sky was streaked
With smoke, and on the playing-field below workmen
Adjusted the display-pieces. She shivered and drew the black
Cardigan over her shoulders. Then, as if by accident,

A shattering flare of metals fell out over the dark
Lake, and cardboard shells of rockets, blackened and twisted,

Lay on the hard-packed, squeaky sand: fierce, concupiscent
Green of copper, ferrous wrath of red and, always
Burning above, the blinding pure white, color of flares,
Still glittered on in combined traces of after-image.
A cry shot up from the clump of shadows by the shore
And Mr. Ellis came running toward us, his hand rather burned,
But stopped and turned to watch as, finally, over the lake

The string of Chinese crackers gave up its family
Of ghosts like an accelerating motor, on the Long
Branch sidewalk, painted bright buff by the sinking sun.
A train whistled in the west toward distant Elberon,
Grass-green Elberon. A staid, inglorious Fourth
Sank into seashore night. Whisked out of the city,
The children lay on the roaring strand, while overhead
All that long summer the Von Hindenburg seemed to be
    hanging
Above the beaches: we Jews pointed into the glaring
Sunlight, up at the long, gray beswastikaed bobbin
While Europe unravelled behind it. But there, amid long lawns,
Fixed to the pivotal green turf of unwinding summer,
I stood still and heard the Fourths of July echo contingently
In the fading, brighter part of the early summer sky,
Waiting for life to explode in the next golden moment,
Waiting for cadence of waiting itself to come to light,
Cracking and bursting, and flaring up into significance.

FIREWORKS

Fire is worst, and fires of artifice thirst after more than
Water does and consume
More than the world: the night within which the world
Turns more brightly than we can even
Guess burns out, while tears in a black
Retina spurn hope of repair and
Flare into smoky whisps.

Whispered desire for firing darkness with history, fleeing
Lights that are strung along
Mirroring darkened waters, hissing itself
Upward, dying in aspiration,
Quenched in night; declaring themselves,
Candles burn down, rockets burn up in
Moments they will outlive.

No light can outlast darkness. But light
Is all we have to live by. Fire plays over creation
But fireworks must do more
Than remind. Out of the earth's heart
Flaming salts fly upward into
Pieces of darkness and spark,
Silence of spaces that trusting, following
Faces expect them to die in.

High in that night
The end comes in a cottony silence,
And then the painful crack begotten of all the unquietness
Yet to be: a death too much like life.
O! like white needles in the mind's dark forests, thrust
Up against the ear-drummed brain
O see, O hear the rocket die!
(Whorls and realms of light leap out, leap
Upward to color, to traces of shape, to life)

Darkness was first
And fire followed in violet, white and
Astonishments of orange, shot at the rim of emerging time,
Widening, as still it is: around
The full moon, high above this wide pavilion, hangs
An interior unpierced
Until the bunched homunculus
Head of one high-arching squib rakes
Down at the sphere, penetrates and escapes inside

The moon,
To the light that bleaches its fire
With the inaudible big bang,
The sudden thudding of shock when created
Pain, reflected in rings of thunder
Becomes an eternal remembrance.

We who have been burned, we who have watched
The sights of firing life, still celebrate
Fire with fire. Bright times
Are remembered in heightened nights
For benched spectators, awaiting streaks of light
Above the grandstand, in the park
In the darkness of wild July. When the past
Burst, erupting into event, the flames
Came hard upon
The explosion, but burnings of celebration
Flare up before the crash. The cranium
Of the world's darkened bowl seems now to crack.

We who have returned, guarding our hearts
From burning memory will not again become
Children bewildered. Wild eyes
Are forgotten, and frightening lights
Are quenched in blanketing darkness. Sheets of fire
And screaming whitenesses of dream

Are redeemed from fear of life by the black
Night of generation itself, by flights
Of upward love
Into your most interior hollows, O my
Sole light, my muse, my mind's uranium
In whose star-pierced urn all my ashes die!

For half of life
Nights came so that I might burn
Like a Roman candle, high inside
The blacknesses of summer.
Then there were fireworks. Flesh
Learns of its half
Of death from the mind's flashbulb white
Coming into being, seeing
Something that must come of all this burning,
All this becoming something other than darkness.

THE NINTH OF JULY

In 1939 the skylark had nothing to say to me
As the June sunset splashed rose light on the broad sidewalks
And prophesied no war after the end of that August;
Only, midway between playing ball in Manhattan and Poland
I turned in my sleep on Long Island, groped in the dark of July,
And found my pillow at last down at the foot of my bed.
Through the window near her bed, brakes gasped on Avenue B
In 1952; her blonde crotch shadowed and silent
Lay half-covered by light, while the iced tea grew warm,
Till the last hollow crust of icecube cracked to its death in the glass.
The tea was hot on the cold hilltop in the moonlight

While a buck thrashed through the gray ghosts of burnt-out
trees
And Thomas whispered of the S.S. from inside his sleeping-bag.
Someone else told a tale of the man who was cured of a hurt by
the bears.
The bathtub drain in the Old Elberon house gucked and
snorted
When the shadows of graying maples fell across the lawn:
The brown teddybear was a mild comfort because of his silence,
And I gazed at the porthole ring made by the windowshade
String, hanging silently, seeing a head and shoulders emerge
From the burning *Morro Castle* I'd seen that afternoon.
The rock cried out "I'm burning, too" as the drying heat
Entered its phase of noon over the steep concrete
Walls along Denver's excuse for a river: we read of remote
Bermudas, and gleaming Neal spat out over the parapet.
In the evening in Deal my b.b. rifle shattered a milkbottle
While the rhododendrons burned in the fading light. The tiny
Shot-sized hole in the bathhouse revealed the identical twats
Of the twins from over the hill. From over the hill on the other
Side of the lake a dark cloud turretted over the sunset;
Another lake sank to darkness on the other side of the hill,
Lake echoing lake in diminishing pools of reflection.
A trumpet blew Taps. While the drummer's foot boomed on
the grandstand
The furriers' wives by the pool seemed to ignore the accordion
Playing "Long Ago and Far Away." None of the alewives
Rose to our nightcrawlers, wiggling on the other side of the
mirror.
She was furrier under the darkness of all the blanketing heat
Than I'd thought to find her, and the bathroom mirror flashed
White with the gleam of a car on seventy-second street.
We lay there just having died; the two of us, vision and flesh,
Contraction and dream, came apart, while the fan on the
windowsill
Blew a thin breeze of self between maker and muse, dividing

Fusing of firework, love's old explosion and outburst of voice.

This is the time most real: for unreeling time there are no
Moments, there are no points, but only the lines of memory
Streaking across the black film of the mind's night.
But here in the darkness between two great explosions of light,
Midway between the fourth of July and the fourteenth,
Suspended somewhere in summer between the ceremonies
Remembered from childhood and the historical conflagrations
Imagined in sad, learned youth—somewhere there always hangs
The American moment.
Burning, restless, between the deed
And the dream is the life remembered: the sparks of Concord were mine
As I lit a cherry-bomb once in a glow of myth
And hurled it over the hedge. The complexities of the Terror
Were mine as my poring eyes got burned in the fury of Europe
Discovered in nineteen forty-two. On the ninth of July
I have been most alive; world and I, in making each other
As always, make fewer mistakes.
The gibbous, historical moon
Records our nights with an eye neither narrowed against the brightness
Of nature, nor widened with awe at the clouds of the life of the mind.
Crescent and full, knowledge and touch commingled here
On this dark bed, window flung wide to the cry of the city night,
We lie still, making the poem of the world that emerges from shadows.

Doing and then having done is having ruled and commanded
A world, a self, a poem, a heartbeat in the moonlight.

To imagine a language means to imagine a form of life.

HUMMING

O summer, summer! somewhere a seventeenth season of heat
Is always exploding in roses; and broods of impulse, feeding
No more on their stored winters, released into later stages
Of being, buzzing, emerge from most of their lives' graves.

These nymphs the winter would perpetuate, secure
In their twigs, but the crash of thundering summer over the
full
Cornfields has plucked from the ground the passionate cicadas,
Free to breed for a week in the maple branches, shaded
From the wide, white sunlight exhausting the best of their
lives, to die
Suddenly, as when the sunlight baked on the singing highway
Is cut by the broad blade of shadow from the planting
Of forty yards of trees at a crossroads perhaps.
Sidewalks in the cool glade of sundown are strewn with shells,
Skulls of the dead nymphs, husks of what are not really selves,
Crunched underfoot, like piles of every dead July
Before a seventeenth summer.
Emerging creatures, surprised
By suddenness of growth cry out as do these bugs
With a humming that sounds to outlive the whole of the long
summer.
It never does. Our overhearing hearts are never inured
To the drone of such a demanding band of musicians, whose
furied
Continuous buzzing drills into our lives, agape
With a pressure that lies somewhere between persuasion and
pain.
Agape. Like a rose unwormed yet, without having tasted of
August
Love, I once in my seventeenth summer exposed all the forests
Of my mouth to the trill of the tireless boring insect, the sweat

Wrinkling the leather of the dentist's chair, defenceless
Against the invasion of pain in the secret places of budding
Eros; the whirring of other summers' eventual flourishing
Deferred to the eternal burr that sounded from somewhere
inside me
And that I believed in my seventeenth summer could never die.
Could pain, finally, like noise, become the condition of life?
Like noises of whitening water roaring into silence,
Always, thus never?
The humming of human time is loud
And crowded with single, unbearable voices, that, hour by
hour,
Blend more into timeless buzzing: the lightning mordent of
high-
Tension wires strung skyward across hot green fields; sixty-
cycle
Hum in the bloodstream of music in crowded, unscreened
rooms,
The language of varying tone and the scream of song
confusing
Its steadying drone; the jammed car horn heard from
stories up
And blocks away, while the slowly-dropping summer sun
Lowers a reddening yolk into its cup in New Jersey.
Even the maddened humming, wordless, always wordless,
We do ourselves, that is never an act of speech, like denying,
Blaming or pledging or lying, nor the raising of voice to
heights
That singing is: this is the business of being. To have heard
These undying cicadas, immortal while yet they live, is to burn
For a time in the moment itself. As the hot convertible,
Humming along the black macadam we all are, disturbs
The avenued peace of trees at the side of the road, the sudden
Noise of a horde of cicadas overcomes the surrounding summer
With a sound louder than life. Then, as our car emerges
From the singing glade into dead, white sun, the silence turns

On like a flipped switch, with a sharp crack of nothing,
Beginning the end of the humming, the humming, the end
  of the humming,
The end of remembering happening somewhere ahead in
  the dust.

THE NINTH OF AB

August is flat and still, with ever-thickening green
  Leaves, clipped in their richness; hoarse sighs in the grass,
    Moments of mowing, mark out the lengthening summer.
      The ground
We children play on, and toward which maples tumble their
      seed
  Reaches beneath us all, back to the sweltering City:
    Only here can it never seem yet a time to be sad in.
Only the baking concrete, the softening asphalt, the wail
  Of wall and rampart made to languish together in wild
    Heat can know of the suffering of summer. But here, or
      in woods
Fringing a pond in Pennsylvania, where dull-red newts
  The color of coals glow on the mossy rocks, the nights
    Are starry, full of promise of something beyond them,
      north
Of the north star, south of the warm dry wind, or east of the
      sea.
  There are no cities for now. Even in the time of songs
    Of lamenting for fallen cities, this spectacular sunset
Over the ninth hole of the golf-course of the hotel
  Should lead to no unusual evening, and the tall
    Poplars a mile away, eventually fading to total
Purple of fairway and sky and sea, should reman unlit
  By flaring of urban gloom. But here in this room, when the
      last

Touches of red in the sky have sunk, these few men,
lumped
Toward the end away from the windows, some with bleachy
white
Handkerchiefs comically knotted at each corner, worn
In place of black skullcaps, read what was wailed at a wall
In the most ruined of cities. Only the City is missing.
*Behold their sitting down and their rising up. I am their
music,*
(Music of half-comprehended Hebrew, and the muddied
Chaos of *Lamentations*)

The City, a girl with the curse,
Unclean, hangs on in her wisdom, her filthiness in her skirts,
Gray soot caked on the fringes of buildings, already scarred
With wearing. North, north of here, I know, though, that she
waits
For my return at the end of August across the wide
River, on a slow ferry, crawling toward the walls
Of high Manhattan's westward face, her concrete cliffs
Micaed with sunset's prophecies of stars, her hardened clay
Preserved, her gold undimmed, her prewar streets
uncluttered.
But here in this hot, hushed room I sit perspiring
Among the intonations of old tropes of despair;
Already, dark in my heart's dank corners, grow alien
spores;
These drops of sweat, tears for Tammuz; these restless
fidgetings,
Ritual turnings northward, away from here where fractured
And gutted walls seem still afire in history's forests,
Toward her, the City who claims me after each summer is over.
Returning is sweet and somehow embarrassing and awful,
But I shall be grateful to burn again in her twilight oven.

Meanwhile the cooling ground down toward the roots of the
grass

Heightens the katydids' scherzo. The men disperse in a grove
Of spruces, while from the distant water-hazard, grunts
Of frogs resume their hold on the late-arriving night,
And the just-defunct chants, never perfunctory, but not
Immediate, have vanished into the familiar unknown.
When the days are prolonged, and every vision fails to blaze
Up into final truth, when memories merely blur
A sweated lens for a moment, night is enough of a blessing
And enough of a fulfillment. See! the three canonical stars
Affirm what is always beyond danger of being disturbed
By force of will or neglect, returning and unstoppable.

SUNDAY EVENINGS

All this indigo, nonviolent light will triumph.

Uneven shadows have fallen out of the darkness that waits,
Continuously created there, as in the whiteness
Of the kitchen two rooms away, icecubes are being made
With a humming of generation. Whether, earlier, it had been
Fine, with sunlight infusing the hints of ice incipient
In the blue air, with promises of gleaming winters
Already trumpeting through the blood and singing *"l'Avenir!"*
Unheard, but pounding somewhere within the inner ear,
Or whether the delaying rains and the two-day-old
Grayness of sky, grayness of generality, had
Spoiled the earlier day for being outside an apartment,
Outside a self—no matter. With night unfolding now
In every corner wherever walls meet or dust collects,
What has just been is obscured. The trickle of time and loss
Condenses along the outsides of things: this icy glass
Sweats drops of terror not its own; this room diffuses
Tiny patches of light through its half-shaded windows
Into the winking, myriad galaxies of all
New York on clear October nights—bits of a brightness

It has not, let alone can give; this world inside
These walls, condensing on the outside of my mind,
Has corners and darkenings quite unimaginable,
But visible as Presences in gray and purple light
At this time of day, of week, of year, of life, of time.
Even the usual consolations of Sunday become
A part of all its general threat: symphonic music
On heavy afternoons; the steam-heat, blanketing
A brown couch and a bridge-lamp and dark bookshelves;
No need for a meal, and too much newspaper to be read;
Rooms around this one, full of what is still undone
And what may never be; the glimpses out at tiny,
Unwise revelations of light, from rooms as high up as this,
Several blocks away. And to put an end to the near-
Darkness would hurt too much—a senseless, widening light
From an unfrosted lamp would do it.
But then what?
Why, blinking. Then numbing to the icy fire of incandescence,
Lidded blinds lowering over the windows that overlook
Darknesses of the Park, this room being all the light
In the world now. And then, perhaps, Sunday will have been
over.

But then what? Oh yes, once, perhaps, in a month of Sundays,
The exciting stars against a clear, cold, black sky
Shone down like promising, wise and truthful splinters of
mirror.
We saw that the light was good, and meteored across
The starlight of high Manhattan to ordered arrangements of
taxis
And blocks of apartments, and parties of frosty eyes like wide,
Entire mirrors, reflecting in joy the twinkling, burning
High overhead at the end of some windy afternoon.

But then what? The next week was full of itself, and ended,
Inevitable, in the darkening late afternoon, indoors,

On Sunday. Ended? Or was it merely the new week's beginning
Come to a bad end? No matter. Whatever ends up like this—
The day, week, year; the life; the time—can't be worth much.
On Sunday afternoons, one can have followed the blackening
Water of the river from eyes along the Drive
And then climbed up a concrete hill to one's own walls
And quietly opened a vein. *"It would be no crime in me*
To divert the Nile or Danube from its course, were I able
To effect such purposes. Where then is the crime
Of turning a few ounces of blood from their natural channel?"
Or the crime of emptying this late-afternoon room
Of all its indigo, not by the light of common
Illumination, but by a long pouring of darkness?
Yes, if it is permitted, everything is. So let it
Be. And let it be night now, at very long last,
A night outside the cycle of light and dark and Sunday,
A night in despite of fiery life, or icy time
That starts its chilling-out of the heart each week at five
Or five-thirty or so on Sunday, when the big, enlightening
  myths
Have sunk beyond the river and we are alone in the dark.

HELICON

Allen said, *I am searching for the true cadence.* Gray
Stony light had flashed over Morningside Drive since noon,
Mixing high in the east with a gray smoky darkness,
Blackened steel trusses of Hell-Gate faintly etched into it,
Gray visionary gleam, revealing the clarity of
Harlem's grid, like a glimpse of a future city below:
When the fat of the land shall have fallen into the dripping
  pan,
The grill will still be stuck with brown crusts, clinging to
Its bars, and neither in the fire nor out of it.
So is it coming about. But in my unguessing days

Allen said, *They still give you five dollars a pint at St. Luke's,*
No kickback to the interne, either; and I leaned out
Over the parapet and dug my heel in the hard,
Unyielding concrete below, and kicked again, and missed
The feeling of turf with water oozing its way to the top
Or of hard sand, making way for life. And was afraid,
Not for the opening of vessels designed to keep
Their rich dark cargo from the air, but for the kind
Of life that led from this oldest of initiations
Ending in homelessness, despondency and madness,
And for the moment itself when I should enter through
Those dirty-gray stone portals into the hospital
Named for the Greek doctor, abandoning all hope
Of home or of self-help. The heights of Morningside
Sloped downward, to the north, under the iron line
The subway holds to above it, refusing to descend
Under the crashing street. St. John the Divine's gray bulk
Posed, in its parody of history, just in the south.
Dry in the mouth and tired after a night of love
I followed my wild-eyed guide into the darkening door.

Inquiries and directions. Many dim rooms, and the shades
Of patient ghosts in the wards, caught in the privileged
Glimpses that the hurrying visitor always gets;
Turnings; errors; wanderings; while Allen chattered on:
I mean someday to cry out against the cities, but first
I must find the true cadence. We finally emerged
Into a dismal chamber, bare and dusty, where, suddenly,
Sunlight broke over a brown prospect of whirling clouds
And deepening smoke to plummet down, down to the depths
Of the darknesses, where, recessed in a tiny glory of light
A barely-visible man made his way in a boat
Along an amber chasm closing in smoke above him—
Two huge paintings by Thomas Cole opened, like airshaft
Windows, on darkening hearts, there by the blood bank.
We waited then and the dead hospital-white of the cots

Blinded my eyes for a while, and filled my ears with the silence
Of blanketing rushes of blood. Papers and signatures. Waiting;
And then being led by the hand into a corner across
The narrow room from Allen. We both lay down in the
  whiteness.
The needle struck. There was no pain, and as Allen waved,
I turned to the bubbling fountain, welling down redly beside
  me
And vanishing into the plasma bottle. My life drained of
  richness
As the light outside seemed to darken.

Darker and milder the stream
Of blood was than the flashing, foaming spray I remembered
Just then, when, the summer before, with some simple souls
  who knew
Not Allen, I'd helped to fill Columbia's public fountains
With some powdered detergent and concentrated essence of
  grape,
Having discovered the circulation of water between them
To be a closed system. The sun of an August morning fired
Resplendently overhead; maiden teachers of English
From schools in the south were moving whitely from class to
  class
When the new, bubbling wine burst from the fountain's
  summits
Cascading down to the basins. The air was full of grapes
And little birds from afar clustered about their rims,
Not daring to drink, finally, and all was light and wine.
I forgot what we'd felt or said. My trickle of blood had died,
As the light outside seemed to brighten.
Then rest; then five dollars. Then
  Allen
Urged us out onto the street. The wind sang around the
  corner,
Blowing in from the Sound and a siren screeched away

Up Amsterdam Avenue. *Now you have a chocolate malted*
And then you're fine, he said, and the wind blew his hair like feathers,
And we both dissolved into nineteen forty-eight, to be whirled
Away into the wildwood of time, I to leave the city
For the disorganized plain, spectre of the long drink
Taken of me that afternoon. *Turning a guy*
On, said Allen last year to the hip psychiatrists
Down in Atlantic City, *that's the most intimate thing*
You can ever do to him. Perhaps. I have bled since
To many cadences, if not to the constant tune
Of the heart's yielding and now I know how hard it is
To turn the drops that leaky faucets make in unquiet
Nights, the discrete tugs of love in its final scene,
Into a stream, whether thicker or thinner than blood, and I know
That opening up at all is harder than meeting a measure:
With night coming on like a death, a ruby of blood is a treasure.

WEST END BLUES

The neon glow escapes from
Inside; on a cracked red leather
Booth poets are bursting
Into laughter, half in
Death with easeful love. They
Feign mournful ballads
Made to their mistresses' highbrows

"Lalage, I have lain with thee these many nights"
For example (but I hadn't,
Really, only once, and
When we got to the room

I'd borrowed from a logician
We left all the lights off,
And so in the cloudy morning
She gasped at the sudden, grey sight
Of the newspaper picture of Henry
Wallace tacked up on the wall)

You bastards, my girl's in there,
Queening it up in the half-light

O salacious tavern!
Festus taught me the chords of "Milenberg Joys" there
Far from mid-western places where red sunsets fall
Across railroad tracks, beyond the abandoning
Whistles of trains.

They've taken out the bar that lay along the wall
And put one in the middle
Like a bar in Indiana
(Not the old Regulator where there were hardboiled eggs)

"Approchez-vous, Néron, et prenez votre place"
Said Gellius, and there I was, skulking like Barrault
After his big dance in *Les Enfants du Paradis*
When Lemaître takes him out for coffee: "Yes, Ma," I said
While the frightfully rare breed of terrier waddled
From lap to lap, ignoring his dish of sorrowful beer.
And later on in the evening, swimming through the smoke,
Visions of others came upon us as we sat there,
Wondering who we were: Drusus, who followed a dark
Form down along the steps to the water of the river,
Always seemed to have just left for his terrible moment;
Gaius in Galveston, setting out for Dakar,
Was never away. As a bouncy avatar
Of "Bye, Bye Blackbird" flew out of its flaming cage
Of juke-box colored lights yet once more, finally

I would arise in my black raincoat and lurch my way
Out to the street with a shudder. The cold and steamy air
Carrying protein smells from somewhere across the river
Hovered about me, bearing me out of Tonight into
A late hour like any other: as when at five in the morning,
Clatter of milk cans below his window on the street
Measured with hushed, unstressed sounds of her long hair,
Her pillowslip, beside his window on the bed,
Suddenly the exhausted undergraduate sees his prize
Poem taking its shape in a horribly classical meter
—So would the dark of common night well up around me
As the revolving door emptied me onto the street.

Salax taberna! And all you, in there, past the third
Corner away from Athena's corny little owl
Hiding for shame in the academic skirt-folds of Columbia,
Alma Mater, who gazes longingly downtown—
All you, all you in there, lined up along the bar
Or queening it up in the half-light,
Listen to me! No, don't!

Across Broadway and down a bit, the painfully bright
Fluorescence and fierce tile of Bickford's always shone
Omnisciently, and someone sad and crazy said
"God lives in Bickford's"

But that was after we had all become spectres, too,
And eyes, younger eyes, would glisten all unrecognizing
As heads turned,
Interrupting the stories innocently and inaccurately
Being told about us, to watch the revolving door make a tired,
Complete turn, as the shape huddled inside it hardly
Bothered to decide not to go in at all,
Having been steered there only by the heart's mistakes
In the treasonable night; by a kind of broken habit.

GLASS LANDSCAPE

The dreadful fields, all bare of images, are swallowing
Each other up as he vainly tries to outrace them; shallow
Ice-ponds glare; of images there are none, for the eye
To see or the ear to convert. Only the barely-whitening
Sky to the east menaces the plains with the possibility,
Even, of change. His eye, widening at the window, filling
The known world, he decidedly desires to be a dweller
There, outside the mind's landscapes, outside the clear shell
Of the eye. *Ai, ai, I, I,* dust in his ego, unwatered
With spring tears, tears at the vision before him, shattering
The patient perspective, the patent nonsense of there being
Such a thing as transparency. Nothing really important
Lies in the scene beyond the travelling glass before him.
He has something in his eye, something unendurable
By way of a speck. The terrible night of burning eyeball
And flushed lid is upon him, the other eye now filled
With sympathetic brine, and the sea-green plush seat, spilling
Over the interior seen before him, even barer
Of the possibility of any images than his bleared
Eye is barred to delights. Appearances have dimmed
Into unimportance, and pain has pared down all the distance
Into a present point. "Importance isn't important,
"What's important is the truth," said the rather important
Philosopher who suffered, for all his pains. Then the tunnel
Under the long, long hill comes, and outside the running
Glass of the dirty train window, the darkness plummets
Across its blank, unblamed gray eye, neither praising nor
punishing.

FROM THE RAMBLE

Gracefully touching hands, the three lost, tiny pools
Laughed across open lips of rock between their basins,
Fringed by the dancing late spring grass that barely moved
To the wind's secret music, to the soft, semi-brave
Flashing of sparrows from the glistening mica phrases
Of the gray margins. Gracing all this, the laughter, the sound of
Laughter from where the waters poured from each pool's face
Away toward its sisters, coursed always gently downward,
        Then finally vanishing underground.

From that high, quiet summit, somewhere above the tired,
Parched slope of Burns' Lawn, no voices and no dancing
Of water came; not even in winter, when the thin, bright
Ice snapped like shining foil underfoot, and a trickle chattered,
Almost as if remembered only from louder splashings;
Almost as if in dream, when the wind's secret silence
Flares up as it did in Avignon when the huge swans, sadly
Imponded in the high park, were frozen somehow, wildly,
        Last winter, in the unheard-of ice.

Even in winter, when that slope was always called
Eagle Hill, for the flexible flights of shining children
Shouting down towards the drive, when bare bushes enforced
No secrecy at the top of the hill, the pools still hid.
Unbidden, once, I crept with my sled through drifts and thickets
And saw the three asleep, still holding hands beneath
The bluish ice. Imprisoned? No more than my eyes, which, stinging
With wind and tears of glare, I lidded down, relieved
        For a dark minute of what I'd seen.

High, high above so many rocks they seemed to lie:
Deep back into the park, beyond the places of

So much adventuring: on chasms of schist, split by
Sheer blows of archaic force, we clambered toward the sun
And dared and chose or sulked alone and sometimes wondered.
Back toward the Ramble, there, as in a hidden garden,
The three of them, ringing the sunlight reflected in their flood
In full spring, dancing, remain beyond the reaches of darkness.
        The ponds, the three, have they departed?

I sought them once in the summer; remembering treacheries
Of remembrance, how what never occurred can usurp the true
Event's privileges, warned that they might not be there,
I climbed upward, in June's more distant margin, through
Tangles of greeny brush toward the places they used
To lie among—past where the twisting path that each winter
Revealed as Snake Hill, white, dangerous and cruel,
Clung to the curving rise, tender, asphalted, innocent,
        Black, in the green of summer's wisdom.

And there they were, still braiding together the rippling water,
Leaping into view as I parted a budding hedge
Like some famous painting one finally sees, abroad,
At the end of a great corridor, bound with a connection
Stronger than merely the old rope of total resemblance
To the reproductions of it one had always known.
As, leaping into view, three graces, dancing, bending
Naked arms in a circle of girl, redeem the mere hopes
        That art books' intimations spoke.

And there they were: the unroaring water flashed, silvery,
And high, hot light shot up from the three shallow bowls,
Surfaces gently amove, one to another spilled:
One giving, one accepting, one returning that flow,
The benefits of the surface, light and awareness thrown
Off them, through the eye, to the overseeing mind—
And all this happening with barely a trace of motion
Across their faces, as if the world had too much light
        Ever to mirror in water shining.

As if the three must be forever almost still,
Fixed like an image so well known that memory
Need never reanimate it even for an instant,
There they were, unchanged, confirmed in their present selves.
Or again: once in another summer, crossing westward,
I entered the Park by an unfamiliar gate, and mounted
A fair rise, crashed through brush, took a wrong path, and ended
Up on that eminence of old at a late, late hour,
Surprised by a distant sound of shouting—

A child's, on Eagle Hill, below my vision—and there
They were, barely enclosed in their modest, open room,
Gaily shaded by hedges interlaced carelessly
With the lowering sunlight. Taken, those unastonished pools,
By surprise, by the wrong approach, they lay as if unperused,
More like themselves than ever, all immediate surface
And rippled whorls of reflection shimmering as if newly
Glimpsed, free of deceit, free of perspective's absurd
Draperies; smiling; and yet concerned.

And all was silence, save for the roaring of the world
In its turning. As once, not long before, the same smiling
Silence hung in the air around my head, unheard,
While far away beyond the bath-houses the wild
Surf slapped out its breath against the beach with sighs
And long, gasping diastoles; for there, before
My wearied eye at the knot-hole, ringed with noon's high sunlight,
The three undressing girls stopped for a moment, awed
By the quiet air and the sun and all.

And there there there they were, grouped in the narrow locker
Within my breathless ring of vision, unbroken circle
Of heads averted, stretched arms, and all motions stopped,
One from the rear, the others facing me and turned

Gently inward, the gleam of skin and shadow of fur
Giving of all their surfaces, phenomena generous
Beyond deserving, as if the good one did were served
With double return, as if one could face the benefit,
        The moments of light now, the given present.

But all in an instant becomes the past, the intermittent . . .
The given is withdrawn. Whether a meteor trail
A following streak of fire or of searing after-image,
Our very glimpse of it consumes what should remain;
Cumulonimbus gatherings aloft in the blue fail,
Falling in the wind, into senseless blobs of cotton;
Tears dissolve a moment into what hearts can make
Merely memorable, perhaps precious, or even solemn—
        A source turned off, a cycle stopped.

And, as the sad rain, falling at four o'clock in the morning
Renews the half-lit hollow streets, and curling smoke,
Emerging from deep beneath shining surfaces, calls
Only losses to mind, only the last sigh-blown
Touch betwixt cloth and skin, only the last condoling
*"See? We've really lost nothing tonight, because life
Is much too complicated,"* only the leaving, and only
Then the continuing rain outside, barely brightening
        Streets, just darkening hearts, finally—

So with the clear-eyed world, freshly washed of vision.
Three naked girls in the shadows of noon, three shallow basins
Open to all the weathers, fall away into flickering
Points of memory, their substance consumed, their surface
    aflame.
They burn, they burn! So in winter once, I began to trace
Them out again by another unfamiliar route;
Thinking again to regain the withdrawn, the radiant spaces,
The flowered moments and points of joy, I sought my pools,
        Cold at my shoulders, the wind, pursuing.

Cold at my feet, the hard, dry ground at the fringes of the
 Ramble.
Here all the surrounding city is hidden; even in winter
When gray mists seem to condense in bare, unfocused branches,
None of the heights of buildings ringing the park is visible.
There among intricate paths, crossing themselves and twisting
Mazy configurations out of the asphalt walks,
Was the heart of the Park, with its dells and bridges over the
 inlet;
There was the final garden, full of the planned disorder,
  Of the garden regained, forced and sprawling.

Cold at my heart, the climbing slowly west and upward,
Away from one Museum with a painted past behind me
Toward the other's boundless pictures—cases of animals stuffed
From which I learned to read all landscapes and to climb
Inside all painted prospects, into their hidden lives.
Cold at my ears, I moved toward the huge, dark halls
Of skull-formed Africa where I had roamed, in childhood,
A wondering traveller along those mental shores;
  Cold at my eyes, I walked and walked.

And there they were, but not as they had been remembered,
Two hardly distinguishable, the third dried-out and muddy,
Misshapen clumps of puddle, they lay, a visionary
Disaster, before me, my eyes bleared and my heart fluttering—
As if the recollected surfaces had sunk
Down into crusty sockets of earth, ringed with sparse and
Dried-out grass, the given presence absorbed by dull,
Treasureless mines that the thirsty, chilling present park's
  Ground all had come to, dark and hard.

Mud at my heart, I could only stare, then turn to the east and
Vanish into the Ramble, losing the misplaced
And badly recollected pools behind me, even
As the city itself was hidden behind the narrow frame

And binding horizons of trees and underbrush. I made
My way across the cold, unfeeling paths that twist
About through the real distances, and finally came
Out of the park, into the unmistakeable city
Safe for the heart, because unenvisioned.

—Not like some misremembered loveliness of trees
Bare, for instance, of leaf in misty February:
Their blackish filaments, plane behind plane, receding
Into the general and dissolving gray, are melted
Down to remembrances of branches, to negatives,
To losses. I coughed in the fumes of traffic, as around me
Windows and parking-lights and other presences
Emitted a world I was hardly grateful for. It crowded
Behind my eyes in that darkening hour.

As if the pools had vanished into the unabsorbent
Ground, I would avoid for months and months thereafter
The eminence they'd lain upon, now always courting
Other corners of path and bench and brush, the Ramble
Springing to green and filling the sky's borders with splashes
Of decoration. Down in some dirty dale, all hunched
Into a fading bench, time after time I sat
Brooding over the few pictures of those sunken
Pools I had kept untorn and uncluttered.

And once I walked toward where I pictured them separated
By clumps of protecting privet, emerging, as once ascended,
In tiers, first one, then, hidden, the second giving way
Immediately to one more, facing off to the west.
Having gained the last height there, I turned toward the setting
Sun, behind the pairs of towers that guard the rim
Of the visible—the modernistic CENTURY, the stubby MAJESTIC
And gold-painted SAN REMO, and uptown at the edge of vision,
EL DORADO'S pinnacles springing

Skyward,—then penetrate the great blue open room
Where all the sunsets burn; downward they disappear
In unseen chambers of bedrock; outward, already ruins
Of a wild, recent time, evoking all their fearful
Doubles in Moscow; branchless stumps ringing a clearing
In irony's forest. But inward, they glow in the dying sun
To cauterize the winds that make them matter and give
Them meaning: all the sad, ugly towers, mortared with mud,
        Moribund, crumbling into dust.

Even at dawn, even at fairer moments than these
Glimpses out at the boundaries of all this ruined garden
Reveal a city to be achieved, the towers unreal,
The glittering windows unapproachable, the far
Finials and fretwork lifted almost to the stars
Beyond even their own vulgarity, beyond
The gestures of aspiration that left them scattered, sparkling
At all the irrational hours, hung high, but yet unpromised
        There where only the eye can follow.

Once even at the false sunset inside the plated dome
Of the planetarium, when night falls far too soon,
The bungled silhouetted mockups of all those
Surrounding towers, unbelievable and crude,
Taught me to watch the slower vanishings at the true
Rim of the park at dusk. At dusk in our present time,
Too, we learn of our sick condition: the senseless, the cruel,
The angry and the deprived roam through the lack of light,
        Smashing the benefits long denied them.

So frowning violence reassumes the crowded land,
And silently, as afternoon unfolds its shades,
Boys with corrupted terriers wander among the Ramble's
Winding and convoluted walks. In the terminating
Spring's convulsive heat, shouts drift up, then fade
Over the nearby water, and even to have remembered

Light leaping up like laughter from three surfaces, breaking
Out of those lost ponds into the shining air, is a blessing.
Have I a right to demand their presence?

I must deserve such benefits, such pools of water, such frail
Surfaces of delight, whether remembered by
Mistake, or really received, deserved not by laboring
Merely, but by a readiness of the heart to accept such fine
Gifts of phenomena. To what have I been entitled?
A loan of three ponds, perhaps. A gift of light over snow
In the glare of December sun. A solemn launch, gliding
Among rowboats. Discoveries of love on dark October
Benches beneath smashed lamppost globes.

—To a glimpse more precious, even, than those of goldenmost towers.
When, once at hide-and-seek, by a path, that ran below
The crown of hill engemmed with ponds that I'd not found
Out for myself yet, I pushed through a hedge of broken
Privet and fell headlong against the concrete and oaken
Bench, where a tall fat man I now guess was thirty-five
Or thereabouts, was stretched, brooding, with his whole
Length extended along the bench, his head supported
Not with his palm, along the jaw,

But on his wrist and the back of his hand, his fingertips
Continuing past his chin; and he lay on his left side
And watched me as I rubbed my scraped brow with my mitten.
And from where I stood, I read on his face the kind of smile,
Awkward, a little strained, that one can often find
In mirrors; and as the wind blew dead leaves on the path
Tangling his long, untidy hair, I turned, and behind me
He lay there motionless. I felt him bless me. I ran
Away from the vision behind my back.

What did he see, that lying man? A boy, running
Down along an airless path between scrubby trees?
Three silent children playing in a ring, then? Something
Utterly different, rising behind his eyesight weeks
Later and then forever? For whatever he had received,
Oh let him have been thankful, even as I am now:
It is a garden we fall from; a city, somehow, we feel
That we have been promised, though not a city built to
surround
A park, a remembered past like ours;

It is a garden inside a city I will have remembered,
And three small pools I will remember having imagined
As gracing the top of an undistinguished eminence
Not too high in that park. Lying now in the grass,
Cool in the light of July on a sward long past
Burns' Lawn, we fasten our tired gaze, she and I,
Across the trees to the west, framing our world in a vast
Moment of stillness. This night, this newly darkened sky,
This scarred park rolling out behind us,

Even this city itself, are ours, wholly unshared
Because unremembered except by both of us, who have made
Light come into darkness, graces dance on a bare
Hilltop, a cycle of months spin around on a frail
Wheel of language and touch. O see this light! As a blaze
Of cloud above the western towers gleams for an instant
Up there! Firing the sky, higher than it should be able
To reach, a single firework launched from the unseen river
Rises and dies, as we kiss and listen.

From Movie-Going and Other Poems

MOVIE-GOING

Drive-ins are out, to start with. One must always be
Able to see the over-painted Moorish ceiling
Whose pinchbeck jazz gleams even in the darkness, calling
The straying eye to feast on it, and glut, then fall
Back to the sterling screen again. One needs to feel
That the two empty, huddled, dark stage-boxes keep
Empty for kings. And having frequently to cope
With the abominable goodies, overflow
Bulk and (finally) exploring hands of flushed
Close neighbors gazing beadily out across glum
Distances is, after all, to keep the gleam
Alive of something rather serious, to keep
Faith, perhaps, with the City. When as children our cup
Of joys ran over the special section, and we clutched
Our ticket stubs and followed the bouncing ball, no clash
Of cymbals at the start of the stage-show could abash
Our third untiring time around. When we came back,
Older, to cop an endless series of feels, we sat
Unashamed beneath the bare art-nouveau bodies, set
High on the golden, after-glowing proscenium when
The break had come. And still, now as always, once
The show is over and we creep into the dull
Blaze of mid-afternoon sunshine, the hollow dole
Of the real descends on everything and we can know
That we have been in some place wholly elsewhere, a night
At noonday, not without dreams, whose portals shine
(Not ivory, not horn in ever-changing shapes)
But made of some weird, clear substance not often used for
gates.
Stay for the second feature on a double bill
Always: it will teach you how to love, how not to live,
And how to leave the theater for that unlit, aloof
And empty world again. "B"-pictures showed us: shooting

More real than singing or making love; the shifting
Ashtray upon the mantel, moved by some idiot
Between takes, helping us learn beyond a trace of doubt
How fragile are imagined scenes; the dimming-out
Of all the brightness of the clear and highly lit
Interior of the hero's cockpit, when the stock shot
Of ancient dive-bombers peeling off cuts in, reshapes
Our sense of what is, finally, plausible; the grays
Of living rooms, the blacks of cars whose window glass
At night allows the strips of fake Times Square to pass
Jerkily by on the last ride; even the patch
Of sudden white, and inverted letters dashing
Up during the projectionist's daydream, dying
Quickly—these are the colors of our inner life.

Never ignore the stars, of course. But above all,
Follow the asteroids as well: though dark, they're more
Intense for never glittering; anyone can admire
Sparklings against a night sky, but against a bright
Background of prominence, to feel the Presences burnt
Into no fiery fame should be a more common virtue.
For, just as Vesta has no atmosphere, no verdure
Burgeons on barren Ceres, bit-players never surge
Into the rhythms of expansion and collapse, such
As all the flaming bodies live and move among.
But there, more steadfast than stars are, loved for their being,
Not for their burning, move the great Characters: see
Thin Donald Meek, that shuffling essence ever so
Affronting to Eros and to Pride; the pair of bloated
Capitalists, Walter Connolly and Eugene Pallette, seated
High in their offices above New York; the evil,
Blackening eyes of Sheldon Leonard, and the awful
Stare of Eduardo Cianelli. Remember those who have gone—
(Where's bat-squeaking Butterfly McQueen? Will we see again
That ever-anonymous drunk, waxed-moustached, rubber-legged
Caught in revolving doors?) and think of the light-years logged

Up in those humbly noble orbits, where no hot
Spotlight of solar grace consumes some blazing hearts,
Bestowing the flimsy immortality of stars
For some great distant instant. Out of the darkness stares
Venus, who seems to be what once we were, the fair
Form of emerging love, her nitrous atmosphere
Hiding her prizes. Into the black expanse peers
Mars, whom we in time will come to resemble: parched,
Xanthine desolations, dead Cimmerian seas, the far
Distant past preserved in the blood-colored crusts; fire
And water both remembered only. Having shined
Means having died. But having been real only, and shunned
Stardom, the planetoids are what we now are, humming
With us, above us, ever into the future, seeming
Ever to take the shapes of the world we wake to from dreams.

Always go in the morning if you can; it will
Be something more than habit if you do. Keep well
Away from most French farces. Try to see a set
Of old blue movies every so often, that the sight
Of animal doings out of the clothes of 'thirty-five
May remind you that even the natural act is phrased
In the terms and shapes of particular times and places.
Finally, remember always to honor the martyred dead.
The forces of darkness spread everywhere now, and the best
And brightest screens fade out, while many-antennaed beasts
Perch on the housetops, and along the grandest streets
Palaces crumble, one by one. The dimming starts
Slowly at first; the signs are few, as "Movies are
Better than Ever," "Get More out of Life. See a Movie" Or
Else there's no warning at all and, Whoosh! the theater falls,
Alas, transmogrified: no double-feature fills
A gleaming marquee with promises, now only lit
With "Pike and Whitefish Fresh Today" "Drano" and "Light
Or Dark Brown Sugar, Special." Try never to patronize
Such places (or pass them by one day a year). The noise

Of movie mansions changing form, caught in the toils
Of our lives' withering, rumbles, resounds and tolls
The knell of neighborhoods. Do not forget the old
Places, for everyone's home has been a battlefield.

I remember: the RKO COLONIAL; the cheap
ARDEN and ALDEN both; LOEW'S LINCOLN SQUARE'S bright shape;
The NEWSREEL; the mandarin BEACON, resplendently arrayed;
The tiny SEVENTY-SEVENTH STREET, whose demise I rued
So long ago; the eighty-first street, sunrise-hued,
RKO; and then LOEW'S at eighty-third, which had
The colder pinks of sunset on it; and then, back
Across Broadway again, and up, you disembarked
At the YORKTOWN and then the STODDARD, with their dark
Marquees; the SYMPHONY had a decorative disk
With elongated 'twenties nudes whirling in it;
(Around the corner the THALIA, daughter of memory! owed
Her life to Foreign Hits, in days when you piled your coat
High on your lap and sat, sweating and cramped, to catch
"La Kermesse Heroique" every third week, and watched
Fritz Lang from among an audience of refugees, bewitched
By the sense of Crisis on and off that tiny bit
Of screen) Then north again: the RIVERSIDE, the bright
RIVIERA rubbing elbows with it; and right
Smack on a hundredth street, the MIDTOWN; and the rest
Of them: the CARLTON, EDISON, LOEW'S OLYMPIA, and best
Because, of course, the last of all, its final burst
Anonymous, the NEMO! These were once the pearls
Of two-and-a-half miles of Broadway! How many have paled
Into a supermarket's failure of the imagination?

Honor them all. Remember how once their splendor blazed
In sparkling necklaces across America's blasted
Distances and deserts: think how, at night, the fastest
Train might stop for water somewhere, waiting, faced
Westward, in deepening dusk, till ruby illuminations

Of something different from Everything Here, Now, shine
Out from the local Bijou, truest gem, the most bright
Because the most believed in, staving off the night
Perhaps, for a while longer with its flickering light.

These fade. All fade, Let us honor them with our own fading
  sight.

ARISTOTLE TO PHYLLIS

for Rogers Albritton

(The 14th century legend of Aristotle and the girl sometimes called Campaspe exemplified the frailty of pagan learning and the power of Amor. Represented in medieval sculpture by a beaming court-lady astride a solemn scholar, the story is later illustrated by a modish whore forcing a nasty old man to carry her piggy-back in the work of Northern engravers like Urs Graf, Baldung Grien and Lucas Van Leyden around the turn of the sixteenth century. The speaker in this poem is a composite of the medieval cleric and the lascivious humanist of the later pictures. Meden agan: *the famous "nothing in excess" of the Greeks.)*

This chair I trusted, lass, and I looted the leaves
  Of my own sense and of clerks' learning, lessened
The distance towards the end of my allotted eyesight
  Over dull treatises on Reason and
Sensuality, learning very little about
  What can still happen on a summer morning.
Faint sea-breezes, when felt too far inland, sometimes
  Smack bone-deep, bruise marine depths, somersault
Into a flood of sick sea-longing. You walked past
  The window where my writing desk stands thick
And oaken, jammed against the mullioned lights, and where
  A pitch pine litters all my work with fragrance
Once too often. If all beauty is scale and order,
  Well then, the old man is unbeautiful
In outraging his age, that should be past all dancing,
  Playing all too well the infidel sage
Unwilling even to gamble on a Final Life
  That is no sleep. And this being so, a simple
Country matter can be so urgent, and a piece
  Of tumble, bubbly breasts and trollopy

Lurch, can matter so much. So little can be said
For you, except that you're alive. But such
A question, with the right wind freshening from the sea
Blows back and forth across the mind: the bright
Emphatic mosses, furring the cracks along the garden
Wall, trembling in the touch of breeze and blurring
The surface of the masonry, fill all the sight.
But still, trained in restraint and reared in reason,
I sit at my desk, half in death, and staring down at
A wide papyrus, silenced, blanched and deafened
To pleas for eloquence, its face pale with long darkness:
Some other age must smash its last defense.
We're no historians; what's past has faded, died, and
Lingers no more; and only its remains
Appear in patchworks of quotation, as in all
The fussy, fretted centos that I have
Assembled from the poets. Even here (and you
Must get the scribe who reads you this to show
Them all to you) the tessellated lines of one
Whose greatest voyages involved the vessel
From which he dipped pale ink of an exotic nature,
Appear; but in my language all these sink
Into an earthier journey. A few swift rounds
Under the evergreens outside; the fir
And box-hedge hiding us, clouds peering in the pool
To view gardens reflected, and the yews
Along the wall waving green, encouraging brushes;
Come, Phyllis, come; the miles I have been saving
Are for your travelling. Only in middle age
Did *meden agan* amount to anything.
Come away! pass the mead again; and gathering
Your thick skirts bellyward, lean back and lead
Me, simpering, outside into the garden. There
As you throw up your leg to climb astride
My back, I'll dutifully munch the bit; then bottom
To bottom, will the no-backed beast run, duly

Peripatetic at each mossy garden corner.
   Giddyap, good Doctor! If by chance the static
And pungent waters of the garden pool reveal
   Our natures to our eyes, it's all part of
The party, eh? Stammering, balanced, the master
   Of those who know, old staggerer, not bearing
A chubby giggling slut merely, but rather, like
   Some fabled, prudent beast that bears with it
Its water, nutriment or home, will carry then
   The bed he'll soon board. Underneath a tent
Of cherried branches ripening fast, I'll put you to
   The plow, and turn your furrows up, and Spring,
Spring will envelop all the air. From far across
   The wall a scent of distant pines will fall
Even as now it drops across my writing desk,
   Full of reports of distant life, and hopes
Regained, and projects floated on an unnavigable
   Future. And whether there will be a fated
Sea fight tomorrow, exploding, showering results
   On the ignoring water, or merely a plodding
And serious fool about to quarrel with a colleague
   Over what once I might have meant (devout
Enough, both of them, although never having learned
   The tongue I write in) cannot be told now.
But at the brink of the moment, mad, mad, for its coming,
   Our knowledge quickens, ripping at the garment
That cloaks the truth that will be. Let's get on with it,
   The game in which the master turns the silly
Ass, straining for breath, arousing the outraged gales of
   What should have been a season of calm weather.

THE ALTARPIECE FINISHED

for Philip Guston

I cannot see how in time it will be possible to look at
it without making all kinds of mistakes: not so much about what
means what, or about how it all was done (subtly, Oh quite subtly
enough) but just in thinking that something need be said at all. The
meaning, taken from the old books—both may disappear under the
raucous, continuing crackle and the hushed scuffings of age.

The light may go, too; and the light was always what seemed
 to matter
most, here in the North: a gray pond with five tiny figures
 gliding
over it; a street with a pair of burghers discussing something
underneath the Sign of the Ram's Head—to see these things in
 the thin, bright
glaze of daylight through the opened window was forever to be
reminded that winter's glare would finally shiver into the fine
thousand shards of warming, brilliant summer, that the endless,
 dark night
immanent and imminent both, had, after all, not come just yet.

Even if all this brightness falls to a yellowing gloom, what will
always matter most will remain. There is only one way to look
at it: open it, and a world is displayed. Close it, and a
room is made manifest, a most peculiar enclosure, through the
window of which lies the world. But folded inside is the painted
world. The whole is subtly done. The doing has eaten away more
than time, or a great biblical golden talent of invention.

Shhh! Having it opened and closed for you is to be before it
in the right way; as the panels creak, heavily, open, shut, I
think of all the other times when watchers will have to watch
 and say

nothing: when they will some day confront in turn new
silences, the

thing that sits so solidly there made of wood and glass and
wires
waiting—all you have to do is turn the handle and it
twitters . . .

bit of outdoor gaiety, dwarfed by looming, threatening clouds
and green
cumulus foliage, where the swing swings up high, bearing
Climène
over everyone, and, see! in her highest upheld hand, higher
even than her hat, a rose; and down below—shhh!—Lisette
watches,
through a delicate telescope, what? the rose? or (watching for us,
outside the frame) the underthings? Watch, and decide it for
yourself . . .

only serious pink and white picture that there is, that stands at
ends of galleries like some famous accident, waiting for you to
recognize it as the one that took so long to do that its cold
completion was a sorry lot, a thin layer of beggars' joys . . .

But what is time? something paintings take to finish, or to rot, or
to become the way things look in. Time devours. I know
about it.
My name was Hubert Van Eyck and I may not have existed but
now I am the food of worms. Stand quietly before what Jan and
I have done; you can see it on the sixth of May. It will eat you.

HOBBES, 1651

When I returned at last from Paris hoofbeats pounded
   Over the harsh and unrelenting road;
It was cold, the snow high; I was old, and the winter
   Sharp, and the dead mid-century sped by
In ominous, blurred streaks as, brutish, the wind moaned
   Among black branches. I rode through a kind
Of graceless winter nature, bled of what looked like life.
   My vexing horse threw me. If it was not safe
In England yet, or ever, that nowhere beneath the gray
   Sky would be much safer seemed very plain.

DIGGING IT OUT

The icicle finger of death, aimed
At the heart always, melts in the sun
But here at night, now with the porchlight
Spilling over the steps, making snow
More marmoreal than the moon could,
It grows longer and, as it lengthens,
Sharpens. All along the street cars are
Swallowed up in the sarcophagous
Mounds, and digging out had better start
Now, before the impulse to work dies,
Frozen into neither terror nor
Indifference, but a cold longing
For sleep. After a few shovelfuls,
Chopped, pushed, then stuck in a hard white fudge,
Temples pound; the wind scrapes icily
Against the beard of sweat already
Forming underneath most of my face,

And halting for a moment's only
Faltering, never resting. There is
Only freezing here, no real melting
While the thickening silence slows up
The motion of the very smallest
Bits of feeling, even.
                                        Getting back
To digging's easier than stopping.
Getting back to the unnerving snow
Seems safer than waiting while the rush
Of blood inside one somewhere, crazed by
The shapes one has allowed his life to
Take, throbs, throbs and threatens. If my heart
Attack itself here in the whitened
Street, would there be bugles and the sound
Of hoofbeats thumping on a hard-packed,
Shiny road of snow? Or is that great
Onset of silences itself a
Great white silence? The crunching of wet
Snow around my knees seems louder, now
That the noises of the fear and what the
Fear is of are louder too, and in
The presence of such sounding depths of
Terror, it is harder than ever
To believe what I have always heard:
That it feels at first like spasms of
Indigestion. The thought, as one shoves
Scrapingly at the snow that always
Seems to happen to things and places
That have been arranged just so, the thought
Of being able to wonder if
Something I'd eaten had disagreed
With me, the while waiting to die, is
Ridiculous. "Was it something I
Felt?" "Something I knew?" "Something I was?"
Seem more the kind of thing that one might

Wonder about, smiling mildly, as
He fell gently no great distance to
The cushioning world that he had dug.
Silently—for to call out something
In this snow would be to bury it.
And heavily, for the weight of self
Is more, perhaps at the end, than can
Be borne.
                    No, it is only now, as
I urge the bending blade beneath a
Snow-packed tire for what I know can
Not be the last time that I whimper:
I hate having to own a car; I
Don't want to dig it out of senseless
Snow; I don't want to have to die, snow
Or no snow. As the wind blows up a
Little, fine, white powders are sprinkled
Across the clear windshield. Down along
The street a rustle of no leaves comes
From somewhere. And as I realize
What rest is, pause, and start in on a
New corner, I seem to know that there
Is no such thing as overtaxing,
That digging snow is a rhythm, like
Breathing, loving and waiting for night
To end or, much the same, to begin.

A LION NAMED PASSION

". . . the girl had walked past several cages occupied by other lions before she was seized by a lion named Passion. It was from his cage that keepers recovered the body."
THE NEW YORK TIMES, *May 16, 1958*

Hungering on the gray plain of its birth
For the completion of the sunny cages
To hold all its unruly, stretching forth
Its longest streets and narrowest passages,
The growing city paws the yielding earth,
And rears its controlling stones. Its snarl damages
The dull, unruffled fabric of silences
In which the world is wrapped. The day advances
And shadows lengthen as their substances
Grow more erect and rigid, as low hearth
And high, stark tower rise beneath the glances
Of anxious, ordered Supervision. North
Bastion and eastern wall are joined, and fences
Are finished between the areas of Mirth
And the long swards of Mourning. Growth manages
At once vigor of spurts, and rigor of stages.

If not the Just City, then the Safe one: sea
And mountain torrent warded off, and all
The wildest monsters caged, that running free,
The most exposed and open children shall
Fear no consuming grasp. Thus the polity
Preserves its fast peace by the burial
Of these hot barbarous sparks whose fiery, bright
Eruption might disturb blackness of night
And temperateness of civil love. The light
Of day is light enough, calm, gray, cozy
And agreeable. And beasts? The lion might

Be said to dwell here, but so tamed is he,
—Set working in the streets, say, with no fright
Incurred by these huge paws which turn with glee
A hydrant valve, while playing children sprawl
And splash to the bright spray, dribbling a shiny ball—

So innocent he is, his huge head, high
And chinny, pointed over his shoulder, more
A lion rampant, blazoned on the sky,
Than monster romping through the streets, with gore
Reddening his jaws; so kind of eye
And clear of gaze is that sweet beast, that door
Need never shut, nor window bar on him.
But look! Look there! One morning damp and dim
In thick, gray fog, or even while the slim
And gaily tigering shadows creep on by
The porch furniture on hot noons, see him
Advancing through the streets, with monstrous cry,
Half plea, half threat, dying in huff of flame!
This must be some new beast! As parents spy,
Safe, from behind parked cars, he damps his roar—
It is the little children he is making for!

When elders, not looking at each other, creep
Out of their hiding places, little men,
Little women, stare back, resentment deep
Inside their throats at what had always been
A Great Place for the Kids: infants asleep
And growing, boys and girls, all, all eaten,
Burned by the prickly heat of baby throbbing,
Already urging scratching hands; the sobbing
After certain hot hurts in childhood; stabbing
Pulses and flashing floods of summer that leap
Out, in the dusk of childhood, at youth, dabbing
At the old wounds from which fresh feelings seep.
"O help me! I am being done!" the bobbing

Hip and awakened leg, one day, from heap
Of melting body call. Done? No, undone!
Robbing the grave of first fruits, the beast feeds again.

Burning is being consumed by flaming beasts,
Rebellious and unappeasable. The wind
Of very early morning, finally, casts
A cool sweet quenching draught on hunger's end,
Those ashes and whitened bones. Each day, to lists
Of dead and sorely wounded are assigned
The tasks of memory. Mute crowds push by
The useless cages and restraining, high,
(But not retaining) walls. Against the sky
Only these ruins show at dawn, like masts,
Useless in ships becalmed, but hung with dry
Corpses, or like unheeded fruit that blasts
High in trees, wasted. Menacing, wild of eye,
The city, having missed its spring, now feasts,
Nastily, on itself. Jackals attend
The offal. And new cities raven and distend.

OFF MARBLEHEAD

A woeful silence, following in our wash,
fills the thick, fearful roominess, blanketing
bird noise and ocean splash; thus, always
soundlessly, rounding the point we go

gliding by dippy, quizzical cormorants.
One black maneuver moving them all at once,
they turn their beaks to windward then, and,
snubbing the gulls on the rocks behind them,

point, black, a gang of needles against the gray
dial sky, as if some knowledge, some certainty
could now be read therefrom. And if we
feel that the meter may melt, those thin necks

droop, numbers vanish from the horizon when
we turn our heads to scribble the reading down
on salty, curled, dried pages, it is
merely our wearied belief, our strained and

ruining grasp of what we assume, that blurs
our eyes and blears the scene that surrounds us: tears
of spray, the long luff's reflex flapping,
crazy with pain, and the clenching sheet,

and, looming up, Great Misery (Named for whose?
When?) Island. Groaning, jangling in irons, crews
of gulls still man a rolling buoy not
marked on our charts. Overhead, the light

(impartial, general, urging of no new course)
spares no approving brightening for the sparse
and sorry gains of one we hold to
now, ever doubting our memory. But

no matter—whether running before the wind
away for home, or beating against the end
    of patience, toward its coastline, still the
        movement is foolishly close to one of

flight, the thick, oily clouds undissolving, crowds
of sea birds, senseless, shrill, unappeased, no boats
    about, and, out to sea, a sickening,
        desperate stretch of unending dark.

RACE ROCK LIGHT

Over sparkling and green water, the lighthouse seems
Smaller than what the sun, pouring about our cupped,
    Shading hands, should contract it
        To; and glaring reflections, splashed

Off the top of the bright bay just at noon are like
Guarding pulses that cut visions to size, adjust
    Shapes of images, lest they
        Seem to matter too much in fresh

Sunlight shining across prospects of summer shores'
Middle distances. Set out on a lump of wet
    Rock, a commonly ugly
        House, mansarded and squat, affronts

Any view of the bay; crowded inside a space
Far too small to surround it, the unlikely house
    Carries, stuck in its roof, a
        Lantern, just as if any fool

Knew "a house plus a light equals a lighthouse." (Eyes,
Minds and voices surmount ignorant bodies, and crowd
Out on top just as oddly,
Though) Remembering times one got

Close to there in a boat, straining against the cold
Wind at sundown to see what he could see, one feels
Puzzled over the keepers
Living here in a house at sea.

Lighthouse-keeping is like gardening here, inside
Narrow confines of rock, water and sky: the sod
Growing thick in the perfect
First of gardens was never churned

Harder than the alarmed Sound in the rake of harsh
Squalls; and Adam could earn Paradise as he served
No more wisely and well than
Those who were planted here to tend

Garden, beacon and house. Reddening, now, and proud
Past enduring, that house looks at the sundown hour
Even more like the scene of
That original dying dream:

Where those beautiful first children are taking turns
Playing being two bad parents, the sunset fast
Making green all the shadows,
Picking out in the window glass

Children's faces, who wait deep in neglect, for rain,
Pouring down on the yard, sending the two ungarbed
Figures into the house once
More, where shadows are always brown,

Their light housekeeping doomed always to leave each room,
House or garden or land messier than the last,
Finally ending with such a
Place as this one toward evening. Shut

Into houses that keep whatever gardens they need
Locked inside their own walls, herded on rocks that force
Heavy currents to race on
By, at least for a while, we make

All our moments of light justify the despised
Houses holding aloft lenses that turn toward shores
Ranged behind them in darkness,
Leaving them with a dying mark.

199

UPON APTHORP HOUSE

The master's residence of Adams House, Harvard: built 1761; —owned privately until 1930.

for Ben and Helen Brower

Introductory

Within this narrow frame expect
No marvels to remain erect
When, crumpled all about this page,
Lie fragments of its ruined age
Whose modes of diction gave assent
To stuffing empty compliment
With feelings of the complex kind
For which this verse was first designed.

How can the stately, white expanse
Immured in my remembered glance
Be folded up in the confines
Of all these short and rigid lines?
Here just proportioning is
Cast in distorting images:
Surely a long façade must shun
Such an obtuse projection.

An isometric view would place
These features in their proper face
And mark, limned with a supple wrist,
Details that blur beneath my fist.
Some flexibility is prior
To what straight renderings require
And true perspective only shows
Through the elastic lines of prose.

A warm, fond photograph may freeze
Split moments for eternities;
The camera's eye may swear an oath
To honor truth and beauty both,
But once in darkness, quite defaults
For thirty grains of silver salts:
Scratch any portrait, and prepare
To find a treacherous snapshot there.

And so an older painter's art
May have to serve to set apart
This house from what surrounds it, then
Assemble house and grounds again
Into one panoramic view,
As a John Vanderlyn could do
Of huge Versailles, a Pugin cage
A macrocosm in a page.

And so a style of graven line
I'd never make completely mine
Must mark this prospect out, and show
How sun or clouded gray or snow
Or fading leaf, or summer rain
Each leaves its temporary stain
Upon that white façade and all
Its dark, high, red surrounding wall.

Red, black and white, and, often, green
Are shades that dominate this scene;
But how to show the barely cast,
Pale dumb penumbra of the past
That rings this house about, and lends
A kind of aging that descends
On all the younger buildings sprung
Around it, which it hides among?

Where courts of Adams House now crowd
Their walls and entries, once their bowed
Troops of green, genuflecting trees
Bending on topiary knees;
And sward and pasture, fence and hedge
Led, sloping, to the water's edge,
Giving the genius of the place
A painted landscape for a face. . . .

Seasons of Apthorp House

Most seasons serve this prospect well:
The whitest of fresh snows dispel
The snaps of cold they usher out
By wrapping all the streets about
In their warm, half-embarrassing shawl,
Familiar and pictorial.
Red fall is far more painterly,
But late spring rains are best to see:

. . . and of Adams

Under their glistening, wet gleam
The cast of all that brick must seem
Less like the red of clay and mud
Than the dark color of our blood;
Their drops, still falling in the wind
Sprinkle the crowns of ivy, pinned
Against each window-pane that grieves
With green tears, in a flood of leaves.

But all these changes only chime
Inside a tiny range of time;
Each season which succeeds the last
Recedes, like feelings in one's past,
Into a darkness—single, white
Instants that flash by like each light
In subway tunnels, having fled
Beyond the eye, inside the head.

Seasons and instants! Dreams and years!
A picture of a house appears
Whiter than any winters are
Or, in time's greener series, far
More shaded than a house can be
By living shrub or natural tree:
Yet in an instant it can mime
The moment of a mass of time.

Seconds and instants! What we feel
At points of being seems more real
Than what we can reflect upon:
Today's mad moment, when the sun
In some *piazza* blinds our sight
On leaving the dark *calle,* quite
Eclipses everything we learned
Yesterday, when our vision burned.

Moments and heartbeats! Glimpses of
Elusive worlds too bright to love,
Too suddenly revealed to touch
And, in the end, not worth too much:
Streetlamps reflected in the ice;
Twilight behind pale fields of rice;
A white house in a dream of trees—
Time is not made of points like these. . . .

The Environs

The ruby Harvard houses, set
In bezels of black violence, get
A kind of brilliance from the light
That needles through the darkest night,
But suffer, somehow, to be dimmed
By grim, suspicious Cambridge, trimmed
Of lamp (except for sections west),
Shaken of superflux, at best.

Black leather jackets by the dark,
Still water of the Charles now mark
The moving present, as they creep
Upon a past that's half-asleep.
Brick and wrought-iron only see
Unhappy gangs, for whom to be
American's a simple fate,
Mutter outside a complex gate.

The Grave of Henry James, O.M.

—While, rotting on Mt. Auburn hill
A presence which invades us still
(His tombstone's name unknown to those
Who rip at undergraduates' clothes
And carve initials in their chests)
If it makes sense to say it, rests,
Beneath that name that's followed by
"OM," like a huge, Vedantic sigh.

T. S. Eliot, O.M.

—While not nearby in London, lives
One more whom history forgives
For having turned from the strong, brown
River of his midwestern town,
Preferring not to think how he
Was complex too, how history
(Reversible as quotations are)
Is now, but is America.

—Not in some English "now" at all:
As hostile Cambridge throws a pall
Of nascent history about
The walls of Adams House, a shout
Of outrage gathers very fast
From all the versions of the past
That, calm and moonlit, always shows
In the white mansion they enclose. . . .

The shapeliest white wooden urn
On a Palladian porch can burn
Like any imitated thing,
Fall to no gentle ruining,
And yield to no romantic cracks:
Time is a trouble that attacks
Its own containers, lays to rest
The minds that get to know it best.

While scholars who affront their lack
Of destiny by looking back
Can hunt for particles of fact,
Their passion passing for the act
Of being an historian;
True history is often done
In dreams: a myth was given where
Young Gibbon pondered in a square.

But dreams bleach out; the dyeing past
Can only keep their colors fast
Through pigment artifacts, that we
May know in fact what used to be.
Seventeen hundred sixty-one
First saw these walls salute the sun:
That vision forces us to think
Of scraps of paper, blurs of ink.

As sparks from a consuming pyre
Of burning paper reach for higher
Positions in the atmosphere,
So tiny troubles cloud the clear,
Sharp, dreamed engraving of the scene
We'd thought to be: this bright and clean
Façade began its frozen waltz
With one East Apthorp's minor faults.

The Builder

East Apthorp, Jesus College, came
Back to his native Boston, fame
Whispering guardedly to him
That, though the prospect seemed quite dim
Across the Charles, the town might be
Illuminated yet, that he
Might start to slake the Church's thirst
With Nonconformist Cambridge first.

This missionary did his best.
Cambridge, alas, was not impressed.
Christ Church was built, but scarcely filled,
While Apthorp started out to build
The splendid house whose very frame
Outlived all of him but his name:
That lived on through our consciousness
Of past in all that we possess.

Ambition called (that Protestant
Eros) a country vicar sent,
In answer, for an architect
Who could, within his cure, erect
The kind of house that might make do
If, just by chance, a mitre blew
In on prevailing winds that led
From London to East Apthorp's head.

The Architect

Newport's famed architectural son,
Palladian Peter Harrison,
Probably built the house—or so
The scholars all conclude, who know
Of various bits of evidence:
The letters, parish documents,
The little drawing from the files
Of papers left by Ezra Stiles,

A college in whose name at Yale
Just now is being built, as pale
Concrete, poured out in wooden forms
Cements the look of gothic dorms
Into a style of some real past
By being modeled on its massed
Gray shapes: new styles arise again
Through history and Saarinen.

(In building we can make it new;
It is not difficult to do.
It's harder to confront the cold,
Keep what we've made from getting old.
Breezes of hopeful spring are filled
With voices urging to rebuild;
Fall winds along the emptied shore
Keep murmuring, "Restore, restore."

Historicism may expand
Our knowledge, but it binds our hand:
The light of what we do, through veils
Of visions of past uses, pales.
So shameless Newport madly built,
Blameless but for our sense of guilt
And Dryden's age, without a smirk
Rewrote Shakespeare to make it work.

But what we envy of such times
Are not that piles of social crimes
Seem cleansed when made foundations for
Their gorgeous relics we adore,
But arrogance beyond defense,
Born of historical innocence
—The Yiddish *"chutzpah"* seems to be
The word that fits it perfectly.)

Firmness, Commodity, Delight
Suffused the rising walls of white
In just proportions (like the State
In dreams we have that soon abate).
No strife divides these goals, nor breach,
In proper houses: each breeds each.
Strength can assure us; beauty wears
Far better than a wall that bears.

Just so, a space that functions well
Dispenses beauty like a bell.
So, too, the Glorious and Profuse:
East Apthorp put this pomp to use
And with each clapboard, foot by foot,
One more aspiring inch was put
On the foundations of his dream
Till it was framed into a scheme.

The lyre's notes were said to cause
Troy's walls to rise, controlled by laws;
If some Amphion built with sound,
Raising divisions from the ground
Then, in the Colonies, he would
Have probably been none too good—
What he built best would be a barn,
All he could handle would be Arne.

But always in an iron age
The golden myths leak off the page
Into reality reversed:
And so these growing walls dispersed
A music of their own, instead,
Rising inside a reverend head.
The tune? *"East Apthorp, turn again,*
Bishop at Cambridge, Rock of men."

The house was built; the town, appalled
By its white wooden splendor, called
It then "The Bishop's Palace," and
When Apthorp left his native land
For England (Autumn, 'sixty-four)
Again, a third and final floor
Was added by the purchaser,
John Borland, merchant, realtor.

Another Owner

—And, as in ten years it turned out,
A Tory. He was put to rout,
Took to another house he had
In Boston, and one day the fad
For watching wars from ringside seats
In milder times worked its deceits:
He watched some soldiers steal some sheep,
Fell from his roof to final sleep. . . .

Then John Burgoyne slept here. The rest
Is anti-climax (so we test
What monuments we have, for age).
While one could cover page on page
With records of its ownership
In later years (who took a trip,
When, where; and who made what repairs)
There's hardly anyone who cares. . . .

Rush on, rush on

So too, the flow of changing shapes
Of life inside this house escapes
The curse of famous happenings
By simply growing old, like things.
As the Republic prospered, so
Fared Apthorp House, which came to know
A nineteenth century of ease,
Padded, stuffed, unashamed to please. . . .

Then finally taken over by
Harvard itself, and helped to fly
Its true historical colors (done
By careful restoration)
In nineteen thirty, it became
The Master's House of Adams, fame
Appended to it on a plaque,
Its comfort as a house brought back. . . .

Abutting on an inclined seat,
It simply sits in Plympton Street,
Assembling without unease
The building of three centuries,
Split and composite, like the world
Of cities that have grown and curled
New regions round their oldest parts,
Guarding, betraying them, like hearts.

In cities that blot out the sun
Moral imagination
Is needed to discern the past
Hidden among the wearied, gassed
And mottled multitudes of lives,
Cut up by steel and concrete knives.
But one need not search far to see
Harvard inside its history.

Thus, moving from a central core
Of builded past, one leaves the door
Of Apthorp House behind, to pass
Along a little bit of grass
Out of a court, across a street
To where the past and present meet,
Quite simply, and in more or less
Of New England revival dress.

One walks through gold, Hispanoid rooms
Past a gray stairwell, wrapped in glooms,
Through which, up one more flight, peers out
Half-glaring, half, perhaps, in pout
(The rendering leaves rather much
To be desired by way of touch),
At generations bred to lead
The greenish visage of John Reed.

The Dining Hall, also Used for College Plays

The portraiture inside the long,
Fine dining hall seems rather strong
On Adamses, as well it might,
And through each day's evolving light
Unchanging, hang their painted forms
Whose jaws and foreheads seem like norms
Or, Wittgenstein so shrewdly says,
Like family resemblances.

(*The House Lights Dim*)

(So, posed with looks that brook no leer
Like the Apollo Belvedere,
Important statesmen used to wait
Above the heads of men of state,
While new decisions would conclude
With grateful glances at the rude,
Aristocratic stares that told
Them of the dignities of old.)

Henry Adams

Their offspring Henry came to know
Which ways the winds of change could blow,
And, worried lest he look grotesque,
He twiddled magnets on his desk,
Hoping that iron filings, spread
Across a sheet of paper, led
To knowledge of the One Big Thing
That made facts all worth studying.

But when he finally thought he saw,
In her thin lingerie of Law,
Half-naked Chaos, all his thought
Forgot what Quincy should have taught:
He gaped and stayed, and, half-repelled,
Half-fascinated, never quelled
His queer desire for her kind
Of barefoot romping through the mind.

His Book

Did Adams try to puzzle out
What history was all about
Or rather merely what it meant
To have been born an Adams, bent
Into a nineteenth century shape
And bound there, hopeless of escape?
The *Education* seems to know
And to pretend it wasn't so.

It moves with irony enough
Through themes that books of stronger stuff
Have often crumpled under, and
Almost appears to understand
That words like "power," "force" and "light"
Are rather dazzling to the sight,
That physics worshipped, like the moon,
Itself turns spooky all too soon. . . .

In Washington he sat and watched
His old friends flicker out, and botched
His clockwork version of the past
And why it speeded up so fast;
He suffered a collapse of will
Before some Fourier integral
That might have comprehended quite
Those waves of epoch, shock and light.

The skeptic, Nietzsche said, made weak *and Others . . .*
With longing, breaks out in mystique:
Adams and others finally turned
Their faces toward the light that burned
Out of the darkling past, or, worse,
Toward the hot southern sun's reverse
Of Northern reason, where the light
Is so hot that it blinds the sight.

The doting Newton no one knows
Hides in an endless list of those
Who, coming to a dotty end,
Take madcap measure to prehend
The universe, or, just as bad,
Equating Beauth and Truty, add
A few odd integers, decide
That Chartres is really worth the ride.

Age, armoring knowledge, cover well
The infant's hopeful fontanel,
While the best, hardest heads we've got
Can ripen only when they rot;
Less fragile than the blasting rose,
Mathematicians decompose
Far more completely than we think,
Like certain mushrooms, dripping ink. . . .

Still, like the urgent cry for light
Of Claudius on opening night,
The Old Philosopher's demand
For a world he could understand
Is like our own eventual call
For "House-lights Up" to end the pall
Of velvet dark, as, all about
The lights of history go out.

So at performances we pray *The Lights Go On in the Dining Hall*
For the less perfect light of day:
Changed perilously to the stage
Of fragile Hotspur's end, or rage
Of shining Dido's tears, this hall
Dons its familiar paneled wall,
Twin domes, and artificial sun
By Bulfinch out of Burlington.

History plays, as Hegel says,
Continuous performances:
Marx adds, as he goes on to parse
These words, "The second time's a farce"—
So with our monuments: their gleam
Betrayed by being what they seem.
It takes the wisdom of the mouse
To master someone else's house.

Sometimes we make it. Living in *You've Done Well, Ben*
A white museum tempts us to sin
Against Imagination, when
The world demands so much of men
With some capacity to choose
Among the shapes of life that use
Us (rather than the other way)
At twilight of the human day.

Farewell then to theatrics! Light
Replaces the rich dreams of night
So that Imagination may
Start learning how to live by day.
Goodbye to history, to styles
Of wilder times, to gorgeous piles,
Houses that look like sets on stage, *No More of All This*
For monuments must act their age.

Goodbye, Old Tunes! Old modes and feet
Were fine for singing in the street
When all New York was now, and when
Imagined history was then;
When styles one had to find could be
The ultimate morality,
I worked progressions on the lute.
Now I must learn to play the mute.

Take care, Old Enterprise! One tries
The ancient models on for size
And leaves them off when he can know
They're more than something to outgrow.
I've learned that time will not be tricked,
So thanks, old habits I have kicked!
And onelie begetters, please go pack,
Old W.H., get off my back!

All the games I've tried to play
Like ladders, to be thrown away
Once the snug tree-house has been gained,
Seem moments now to be explained
And, in the understanding, die,
Blending, like woodsmoke in the sky,
Into the mind with which I make
The world around me come awake:

New York on this warm summer night,
Coming to terms with black and white
And Spanish olive, pays the cost
In what my old West Side has lost. *My City*
Where integrated children play
Nighttown is all abroad by day;
Where flowery *bodegas* thrive
We pluck our death to stay alive.

There are no Apthorp Houses here;
Cambridge—like some forgotten year
I have been troubling to restore
From scraps: a summer by the shore
(But one of many); two dead aunts;
A party where I wet my pants;
A fall and an acquired scar—
Is at my fingertips, yet far.

I've left there. Let it be. It's true
That what my style must answer to
Is really neither here nor there
But in the thick, engulfing air:
"Between the presence of the dead
And of the living in one's head
There isn't much to choose," I learned
From a philosopher who burned.

What Stanley Said

The wide black river, standing still,
Tilted against my windowsill,
Is still the same phenomenon
I met in nineteen fifty-one
Before I left New York to test
My boundaries by heading west
And, four years later, met at last
The eastern Charles, the Western Past.

The Hudson

I honored it. It served me well
While I was learning how to spell
The signatures that time impressed
Upon my visions. When I'd guessed
That I should have to leave it soon,
On a green sward, one night in June,
I sat and hummed and rubbed my brow.
What I saw then confronts me now:

The Charles

That thin, black river, running by
Mirrors, like some impending sky,
The red and white lights of the cars
That stream along below the stars;
Hung in that dark and fluid void
Each seems a man-made asteroid
Or artificial satellite,
O, vision of tomorrow night!

When finally I no longer will
Be able to imbibe my fill
Of Possibility—a cup
Still drained by simply looking up—
When crowds of Objects will exhaust
An emptiness I will have lost,
And noxious lights may bring about
A night, once more, of fear and doubt.

New London—New Haven—New York, 1958–1961

From A Crackling of Thorns

FOR BOTH OF YOU, THE DIVORCE BEING FINAL

We cannot celebrate with doleful Music
The old, gold panoplies that are so great
To sit and watch; but on the other hand,
To command the nasal krummhorns to be silent,
The *tromba marina* to wail; to have the man
Unlatch the tail gate on his cart, permitting
The sackbut player to extend his slide
And go to work on whimpering divisions;
For us to help prepare the masque itself,
Rigging machinery to collapse the household
Just at the end, rehearsing urchins who
Will trip, all gilded, into the master bedroom
And strip the sheets, is, finally, to confess
That what we lack are rituals adequate
To things like this.
                                        We tell some anxious friends
"*Basta!* They know what they are doing"; others
Whom we dislike and who, like queens, betray
Never a trace of uneasiness, we play with:
"No, it could never work, my dears, from the start.
We all knew that. Yes, there's the boy to think of,"
And so on. Everyone makes us nervous. Then,
For a dark instant, as in your unlit foyer
At sundown, bringing a parcel, we see you both
And stifle the awkward question: "What, are *you* here?"
Not because it has been asked before
By Others meeting Underground, but simply
Because we cannot now know which of you
Should answer, or even which of you we asked.
We wait for something to happen in the brown
Shadows around us. Surely there is missing
A tinkle of cymbals to strike up the dirge

And some kind of sounding brass to follow it,
Some hideous and embarrassing gimmick which
Would help us all behave less civilly and
More gently, who mistook civility
So long for lack of gentleness.
                                        And since
Weeping's a thing we can no longer manage,
We must needs leave you to the Law's directive:
"You have unmade your bed, now lie about it."
Quickly now: which of you will keep the *Lares,*
Which the *Penates?* And opening the door
We turn like guilty children, mutter something,
And hide in the twilit street.
                                        Along the river
The sky is purpling and signs flash out
And on, to beckon the darkness: THE TIME IS NOW . . .
(What time, what time?) Who stops to look in time
Ever, ever? We can do nothing again
For both of you together. And if I burn
An epithalamium six years old to prove
That what we learn is in some way a function
Of what we forget, I know that I should never
Mention it to anyone. When men
Do in the sunny Plaza what they did
Only in dusky corners before, the sunset
Comes as no benison, the assuring license
Of the June night goes unobserved. The lights
Across the river are brighter than the stars;
The water is black and motionless; whatever
Has happened to all of us, it is too late
For something else ever to happen now.

221

THE LADY'S-MAID'S SONG

When Adam found his rib was gone
  He cursed and sighed and cried and swore
And looked with cold resentment on
  The creature God had used it for.
All love's delights were quickly spent
  And soon his sorrows multiplied:
He learned to blame his discontent
  On something stolen from his side.

And so in every age we find
  Each Jack, destroying every Joan,
Divides and conquers womankind
  In vengeance for his missing bone.
By day he spins out quaint conceits
  With gossip, flattery, and song,
But then at night, between the sheets,
  He wrongs the girl to right the wrong.

Though shoulder, bosom, lip, and knee
  Are praised in every kind of art,
Here is love's true anatomy:
  His rib is gone; he'll have her heart.
So women bear the debt alone
  And live eternally distressed,
For though we throw the dog his bone
  He wants it back with interest.

For *The Man of Mode*

LATE AUGUST ON THE LIDO

To lie on these beaches for another summer
Would not become them at all,
And yet the water and her sands will suffer
When, in the fall,
These golden children will be taken from her.

It is not the gold they bring: enough of that
Has shone in the water for ages
And in the bright theater of Venice at their backs;
But the final stages
Of all those afternoons when they played and sat

And waited for a beckoning wind to blow them
Back over the water again
Are scenes most necessary to this ocean.
What actors then
Will play when these disperse from the sand below them?

All this is over until, perhaps, next spring;
This last afternoon must be pleasing.
Europe, Europe is over, but they lie here still,
While the wind, increasing,
Sands teeth, sands eyes, sands taste, sands everything.

A THEORY OF WAVES

Having no surface of its own, the pond,
Under the shifting grey contingency
Of morning mists, extends even beyond
The swamp beside it, until presently
The thinning air declares itself to be

No longer water, and the pond itself
Is still for a moment, and no longer air.
Then waking bass glide from their sandy shelf,
And sets of concentric circles everywhere
Expand through some imaginary thing
Whose existence must be assumed, until they meet,
When incorporeal ripples, ring on ring,
Disturb a real surface, as if, with dripping feet,
Some dark hypothesis had made retreat.

THE GREAT BEAR

Even on clear nights, lead the most supple children
Out onto hilltops, and by no means will
They make it out. Neither the gruff round image
From a remembered page nor the uncertain
Finger tracing that image out can manage
To mark the lines of what ought to be there,
Passing through certain bounding stars, until
The whole massive expanse of bear appear
Swinging, across the ecliptic; and, although
The littlest ones say nothing, others respond,
Making us thankful in varying degrees
For what we would have shown them: "There it is!"
"I see it now!" Even "Very like a bear!"
Would make us grateful. Because there is no bear

We blame our memory of the picture: trudging
Up the dark, starlit path, stooping to clutch
An anxious hand, perhaps the outline faded
Then; perhaps could we have retained the thing
In mind ourselves, with it we might have staged
Something convincing. We easily forget
The huge, clear, homely dipper that is such

An event to reckon with, an object set
Across the space the bear should occupy;
But even so, the trouble lies in pointing
At any stars. For one's own finger aims
Always elsewhere: the man beside one seems
Never to get the point. "No! The bright star
Just above my fingertip." The star,

If any, that he sees beyond one's finger
Will never be the intended one. To bring
Another's eye to bear in such a fashion
On any single star seems to require
Something very like a constellation
That both habitually see at night;
Not in the stars themselves, but in among
Their scatter, perhaps, some old familiar sight
Is always there to take a bearing from.
And if the smallest child of all should cry
Out on the wet, black grass because he sees
Nothing but stars, though claiming that there is
Some bear not there that frightens him, we need
Only reflect that we ourselves have need

Of what is fearful (being really nothing)
With which to find our way about the path
That leads back down the hill again, and with
Which to enable the older children standing
By us to follow what we mean by "This
Star," "That one," or "The other one beyond it."
But what of the tiny, scared ones?—Such a bear,
Who needs it? We can still make do with both
The dipper that we always knew was there
And the bright, simple shapes that suddenly
Emerge on certain nights. To understand
The signs that stars compose, we need depend
Only on stars that are entirely there
And the apparent space between them. There

Never need be lines between them, puzzling
Our sense of what is what. What a star does
Is never to surprise us as it covers
The center of its patch of darkness, sparkling
Always, a point in one of many figures.
One solitary star would be quite useless,
A frigid conjecutre, true but trifling;
And any single sign is meaningless
If unnecessary. Crab, bull, and ram,
Or frosty, irregular polygons of our own
Devising, or finally the Great Dark Bear
That we can never quite believe is there—
Having the others, any one of them
Can be dispensed with. The bear, of all of them,

Is somehow most like any one, taken
At random, in that we always tend to say
That just because it might be there; because
Some Ancients really traced it out, a broken
And complicated line, webbing bright stars
And fainter ones together; because a bear
Habitually appeared—then even by day
It is for us a thing that should be there.
We should not want to train ourselves to see it.
The world is everything that happens to
Be true. The stars at night seem to suggest
The shapes of what might be. If it were best,
Even, to have it there (such a great bear!
All hung with stars!), there still would be no bear.

BUILDING A TOWER

It is because of what one has not found—a tan silo pushing up beside the gambrel roof of a stone barn; a square, ruined tower, Frankish, stone, backed on a pine grove and overlooking the hot sand toward the calm blue water; a dark, shingled cupola inspecting the wild, gray sea; an unused wooden water-tank atop a penthouse facing westward beyond the park; an obsolete lighthouse near the mouth of a bay—what one has not been able to adapt, that one has to build. One can plan and plan for years, but in the end the finished structure will always remain somewhat surprising: it will have to seem, always, to have been come upon, in a middle distance, from a dark walk, the wanderer enwrapped in his study of the failing light and what arises within it. It will always have to keep its own distant appearance: even as one looks out, after years of keeping it, through one after another of the windows—toward the fire of sunset, out across the noon fields, into the cold rain dripping from bare boughs—there must be at least one window, however narrow, out of which one can see what one looks toward the tower for. One must be amid all that—dark books shadowing the interior walls, bright vineyards lying toward the river outside—amid what has always been, and will be, beyond.

Notes to the Poems

SPECTRAL EMANATIONS

golden lamp: "Facing the table, near the south wall, stood a candelabrum (*lychnia*) of cast gold, hollow and of the weight of a hundred minae . . . It was made up of globules and lilies along with pomegranates and little bowls, numbering 70 in all; of these it was composed from its single base right up to the top, having been made to consist of as many portions as are assigned to the planets with the sun . . . the seven lamps faced south-east . . ." Josephus, *Antiquities* II, 144–7. Philo of Alexandria declared that the planets corresponded to the lamps in this wise:

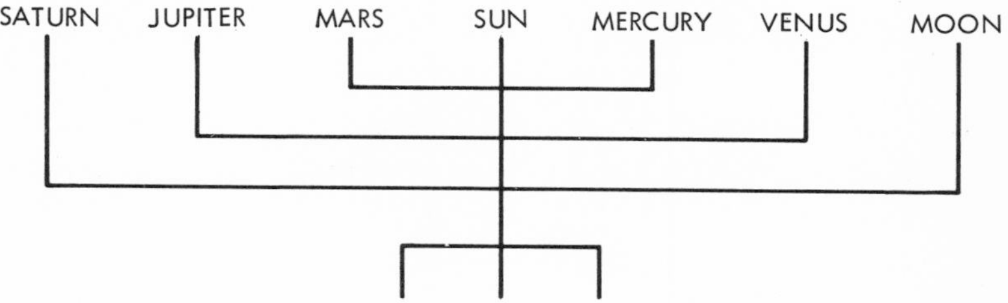

In the text of *Spectral Emanations,* Saturn and Mars have had to exchange their places. There are factorial seven (7!), or 504, lines in the 7 sections of 72 lines each.

THE WAY TO THE THRONE ROOM The original proem was "The Muse in the Monkey Tower" (q.v.); the present one was substituted part way through. The "bright river" is not Chebar, in *Ezekiel* 1:1; the ad hoc angels are named in various mixtures of Indo-European and Semitic. Roy G. Biv, who reappears in YELLOW, is the mnemonic acronym for the colors of our spectrum, and his surname in Hebrew means "sewer pipe".

RED This is the westernmost branch; if such a light go out, the future will be ill (*Yoma* 39b). *A gourd:* the reluctant prophet Jonah sat under one (*Jonah* 4:6) to watch the destruction of Nineveh. The Book of Jonah is read in the synagogue on the afternoon of the Day of Atonement. ("Red" was started during the so-called Yom Kippur war of 1973.) *Parasangs:* Persian units of about 4 miles. *Adom:* like *Adam,* red or terracotta colored; the Hebrew letters that spell both words are derived from pictograms for "ox", "door" and "water".

ORANGE *mere models of the immortal:* as the Mycenaean gold dug up, untarnished. *Gold is gold,* etc.: cf. *Pirke Aboth,* on exchanges. *The painter:* Philip Otto Runge.

YELLOW *Queen of the Peaceful Day:* as Sabbath is supposed to descend on the lit candles on Friday evening as a queen of peace, so the secular sweet day to the daylight lamps of our eyes. *an anecdote:* an illustration of this scene would be a missing painting between *Consummation* and *Destruction* in Thomas Cole's *The Course of Empire* (1836), but the mistaking of Saturn for Mars is always more than a matter of the mechanics of vision. *Hilda:* in *The Marble Faun* of Hawthorne, her copies of the Masters were more exuberant than the sleazy originals of her fellow-artists.

GREEN *Man will nicht weiter,* etc.: Goethe, from the *Color Theory,* ¶801–2; he also observed that yellow was acidic and blue, basic, and adduced this scheme:

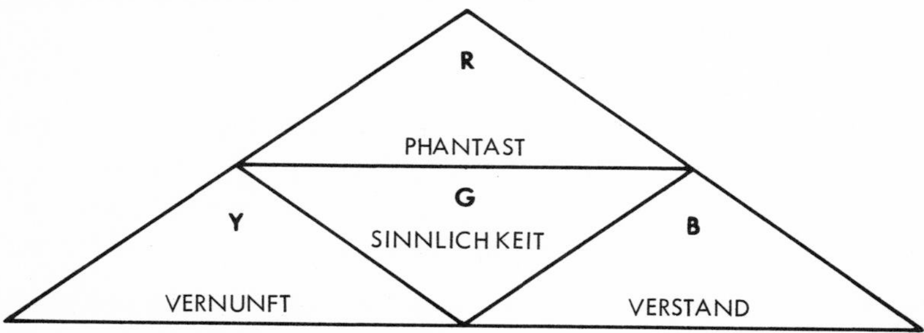

Der begrabene Leuchter: by Stefan Zweig. *Old guidebook:* presumably Hawthorne used this. *seven-faceted stone:* cf. *Zechariah* 4. *Beatrice de Luna:* Doña Gracia Nasi (1510–69), born under her Christian name in Portugal; her story and that of her son-in-law, Joseph Nasi, later Duke of Naxos, are told by Cecil Roth in *The House of Nasi*. *A differently colored lustre:* cf. *Menahoth* 3.6 where the seven branches of the menorah impair each other's validity. *Vespasian's temple of Peace:* at least, according to Josephus, *Jewish Wars* VII, 148–50. *the earth has given its yield:* the end of Psalm 67 sung at the conclusion of the Sabbath on Saturday evening and reproduced, its text patterned in the form of a seven-branched lamp, as an amulet on the walls of oriental homes and houses of worship.

BLUE *Day is naked:* cf. "*Le jour nu même dans ses nuances, ses nuages à genoux, ses ages, ses anges ingénus*" (Ephraim du Blé Engrenier). *No, green:* echoing R. Eliezer, *Berakoth 1.2*. *You had best build one:* this might be entitled "The Contraption".

INDIGO *fragile virgin:* Astraea left us, to become a zodiacal constellation, after the Silver Age, which is why there is no justice in the world, but only in the stars.

VIOLET This is the easternmost point; the labors of Hercules moved westward, hour by hour, but such a course cannot any longer be followed. *inside a pitcher:* according to Cecil Roth, some villagers in northern Portugal were still lighting candles in pitchers on Friday nights, a mere half-century ago, without knowing why they did so save that it was an old family custom. *Ten black drops:* the plagues against Egypt are counted out this way. *three higher colors:* as if the branches have all been lower emanations; there may be three higher ones, a source, a current, a sea, as oil streams into light. *cracked the oil:* "Light is like a niche in which is a lamp—the lamp encased in glass—the glass, as it were, a glistening star. From a blessed tree is it lighted, the olive neither of the East nor of the West, whose oil would well nigh shine out, even though fire touched it not. It is light upon light." *Koran,* Sura XXIV (tr. J. M. Rodwell)

ON THE CALENDAR

The month in question is October, 1929.

THE LADY OF THE CASTLE

Sheelah-na-gig, a kind of obscene carving found on the walls of occasional churches and nunneries in France and Britain. Margaret Murray suggested that they might be instructive anatomical illustrations. The one I invoke is above the clock on the tower of Great Shelford church in Cambridgeshire.

AFTER AN OLD TEXT

Sappho 2; Catullus 51.

THE HEAD OF THE BED

Epigraph: This was a dream; I realized only after having written the 15 sections that follow that the two countries were called, in the language of one of them, sleep and waking. 4 *Vashti:* from the Book of Esther; *Orpah:* from the Book of Ruth; Martha: from the Gospels. 11 *Half his days:* from Sir Thomas Browne. 12: In folk tradition, the skies are supposed to open once a year on the festival of the Giving of the Law. The blind man is like Milton. 13. All these stars are visible in the August sky; before midnight, Cygnus and Lyra are together overhead as a re-collection of the dismembered Orpheus. 14. Chicken Little, in the children's tale, believed the sky was falling; *in vitro . . . in vivo:* as if tested in the lab only or on living subjects. 15 Harold Bloom suggested that the two female personages in this section were really the same. I am now inclined to agree.

THE SHADES

Windowshades, dark glasses, ghosts, degrees of color, shadows, and so forth. *traghetto:* a stand-up, ferry gondola across the Grand Canal.

TALES TOLD OF THE FATHERS

(THE GARDEN) Tiepolo gestures: the sun behaving like the 18th century Venetian painter of theatrical skies.

ROTATION OF CROPS

The title refers both to the method outlined in Part I of Kierkegaard's *Either/Or* and to the nursery rhyme about oats, peas, beans and barley.

THE ZIZ

This creature is very loosely adapted from the one described in Ginsberg's *Legends of the Jews,* Vol. 1, involving also a deliberate mispronunciation of what, in the original, sounds more like "tsits". It is the poem's fancy that the phoenix exists today as the Van Allen belts. The names of the mythical commentators mean "eagle", "dove" and "rooster", in that order.

COHEN ON THE TELEPHONE

I have never actually heard the old phonograph record of the famous dialect-humor routine. The Hebrew phrase *bat-ḳol* (lit., "daughter of a voice") means an echo; the caller's son is Ben Cole because he changed his name from Cohen—an assimilated echo.

GIVEN WITH A GOLD CHAIN

The *only one Golden chain* was the Great Chain of Being, mentioned from Homer and Plato on. The chain given with the poem has since broken.

AFTER CALLIMACHUS

Epigram 41.

A SEASON IN HELLAS

"Kennst du das Land . . . etc."

MOUNT BLANK

Not as high as Snowdon, Ventoux or Niphates. I had not thought of seeing a death on its slopes, but part-way through the composition of the poem, a dear friend, Marius Bewley, suddenly died.

KRANICH AND BACH

The words mean "crane and brook". The last of the Schubert songs in the poem, *Der Leiermann,* is quoted in deliberately stilted Lied-translationese.

THE MUSE ON THE MONKEY TOWER

Like "Ad Musam," this is a kind of spell or prayer for the accomplishment of a difficult task. Hilda, in *The Marble Faun,* lived in the tower here described, in Rome off Via della Scrofa, and sent doves out of the window. Petrarch had himself crowned in Rome with olive, laurel and myrtle. The *tramontana* is a wind that cools hot Roman afternoons.

NEW YORK

Juvenal's exurbanite says "What's there in Rome for me?" This whole verse essay was a contribution to a *Harper's Magazine* series (1970) about going home in America; I had recently returned to New York after 15 years away, thinking never to leave again. I have just this year had to do so. *Whose Moses:* Robert Moses, a man of many projects. *Harrison's foul sway:* the Harrison Narcotics Act, passed 1914. *Wittgenstein:* he frequented the movies. *Director Bing:* Rudolph Bing had then been in charge of the Metropolitan Opera for many years; he has since departed. Thomas P. *Hoving's* replacement at the Metropolitan Museum of Art has not yet been named. John Mitchell was not yet in jail in 1970. Mr. *Koch* is now himself Mayor of New York City. *Lead me not home to them:* It is, after all, from my garden that I add these notes, having been informed that I "shall possess/Metropolis within thee, happier far."

AT THE NEW YEAR

The solar new year starts at the vernal equinox, the academic and Judaic terms at the autumnal one; in the latter instance, apples are dipped in honey and eaten for figurative sweetness.

LETTER TO BORGES

I had just finished translating, at the author's request, Borges' poem on the golem of Prague, in the original meter and rhymes, and I continued in that borrowed vein in order to report to him a Borgesian coincidence.

GRANNY SMITH

This Australian and British apple had just begun to be imported, although it is now common here. *levin:* an old word for lightning.

DAMOETAS

A pastoral name for a former teacher. This poem was written in Cambridge.

VISIONS FROM THE RAMBLE

The Ramble is the section of Central Park in New York City south of the 79th street transverse and north and east of The Lake. From parts of it, none of the surrounding city is visible. WAITING The Fair was the New York World's Fair of 1939–40; Elberon and Long Branch are on the New Jersey shore. FIREWORKS This display is in strict Pindaric triads. THE NINTH OF JULY *To imagine a language . . . etc.:* Wittgenstein, *Phil. Inv.,* I, 19, is here elliptically misquoted. THE NINTH OF AB *Tisha b'Av,* the ninth day of the month of Ab, is a late-summer fast day commemorating the destruction of the Second Temple in Jerusalem, on which the Book of Lamentations is customarily read. SUNDAY EVENINGS *It would be no crime in me . . . etc.:* from Hume on suicide. HELICON *Two huge paintings:* these canvases from Cole's *The Voyage of Life* were indeed hung dimly in St. Luke's

Hospital until about 1955. Neither Allen Ginsberg nor I knew anything then of their artist nor of the rest of the series. WEST END BLUES The West End Bar is on Broadway near Columbia University; some of this section is an adaptation of Catullus 37: *Salax taberna vosque, contubernales.* GLASS LANDSCAPE *Ai, ai, I, I:* Sophocles, *Oedipus Tyrannus* 1308. *Importance isn't important . . . truth:* the late J. L. Austin, quoted by hearsay.

MOVIE-GOING

Written in 1960; time has revised the astronomy as much as the astrophilia, and Mars and Venus are no longer considered to be diachronic versions of Earth. In the *ubi sunt* catalogue of all the theatres that used to line Broadway from 59th to 110th street, I think that I mistakenly added a nonexistent "Alden" to the list.

ARISTOTLE TO PHYLLIS

The quotation from Wordsworth in the last line and the allusion to Aristotle's example of a sea-fight tomorrow were mostly for the benefit of a philosopher friend who had written on the subject of contrafactual conditionals in a controversy currently going on among analytic philosophers. I was also thinking throughout of Mallarmés sonnet, *"Brise Marine,"* and the first line of my poem is a version of the French poem's opening: *Le chair est triste, hélas, et j'ai lu tous les livres.* Lines 6, 7, 9, and 10 of Mallarmé, as well as the title, are all echoed, purely with respect to sound, at various points. Aristotle's advice to the girl to get help in reading his letter to her is well taken.

THE ALTARPIECE FINISHED

The picture is made up, but the inscription quoted in the last lines is adapted from the Ghent Altarpiece. The other paintings in the poem are, in order of appearance, Paul Klee's *Twittering Machine,* the Fragonard swing painting in the National Gallery in Washington, and Philip Guston's *Beggar's Joys.*

HOBBES, 1651

adapts these lines from his own verse autobiography: *Frigus erat, nix alta, senex ego, ventus acerbus; / Vexat equus sternax et salebrosa via.*

UPON APTHORP HOUSE

This started out as a Christmas card for the dedicatees, the master and mistress of Adams House, Harvard, and got out of hand. This is a somewhat cut version. *Is now, but in America:* cf. "History is now and England", T.S. Eliot, *Little Gidding. Firmness, commodity, delight:* Sir Henry Wotton's architectural principles. *Burgoyne slept here:* see the imagined details in R. Graves, *Sergeant Lamb's America. A philosopher:* Stanley L. Cavell

FOR BOTH OF YOU

tromba marina: it was a sort of 17th century single-stringed bass viol; *Lares* and *Penates* were the Roman household gods.

THE GREAT BEAR

Nearly a decade after writing this I came across the following passage from the *Phainomena* of Aratus (fl. 270 B.C.) in re a number of unnamed stars (ll. 370–382):

For they're not arranged like parts of a perfect image
Of something, as are the stars in constellations that move
Along predictable paths as the cycles of time unroll
—Stars that, in the old days, were treated together in figures
Known by the name of what those figures most resembled.
(Back then no one was skilled enough to notice single
Stars, or give them names as individuals.)
There are so many stars! Whirling about the sky
In so many colors and varying degrees of brightness
That ancient sky-watchers needed to notice them in groups,

Patterned and figured together and glimmering into pictures;
And thus the constellations were named, and never thereafter
Could any star rise at night single, and marvellous.

frigid conjecture: Baudelaire likens a cold woman to *"un astre inutile". any single sign . . .* Wittgenstein, *Tractatus* 3.328 and, shortly thereafter, 1.0.

Tuberose
~~rosemb~~ rose-in-bloom
pricket
cocket
Cock socket
fucket — pucker up, little fucket
rose buddy
rosebud
puckerport
pinkyport
prettyportal

JOHN HOLLANDER

John Hollander's first book of poems, A CRACKLING OF THORNS, *was chosen by W. H. Auden as the 1958 volume in the Yale Series of Younger Poets;* MOVIE-GOING AND OTHER POEMS *appeared in 1962,* VISIONS FROM THE RAMBLE *in 1965,* TYPES OF SHAPE *in 1969,* THE NIGHT MIRROR *in 1971,* TALES TOLD OF THE FATHERS *in 1975 and* REFLECTIONS ON ESPIONAGE *in 1976. He has written two books of criticism,* THE UNTUNING OF THE SKY *and* VISION AND RESONANCE, *and edited both* THE LAUREL BEN JONSON *and, with Harold Bloom,* THE WIND AND THE RAIN, *an anthology of verse for young people, an anthology of contemporary poetry,* POEMS OF OUR MOMENT *and was a co-editor of* THE OXFORD ANTHOLOGY OF ENGLISH LITERATURE. *He is the editor (with Anthony Hecht) of* JIGGERY-POKERY: A COMPENDIUM OF DOUBLE DACTYLS. *Mr. Hollander attended Columbia and Indiana Universities, was a junior fellow of the Society of Fellows of Harvard University, and taught at Connecticut College and Yale, and was Professor of English at Hunter College and the Graduate Center,* CUNY. *He is currently Professor of English at Yale.*